Broadway Christian Church Fort Wayne

Discipleship
Swindoll, Charles R.

P9-DOD-434

0000   1915

Discipleship

MINISTRY UP CLOSE AND PERSONAL

BIBLE STUDY GUIDE

From the Bible-teaching ministry of

Charles R. Swindoll

INSIGHT FOR LIVING

PROPERTY OF
BROADWAY CHRISTIAN CHURCH LIBRARY
910 BROADWAY
FORT WAYNE, IN 46802

Charles R. Swindoll is a graduate of Dallas Theological Seminary and has served in pastorates in Texas, Massachusetts, and California since 1963. He has served as senior pastor of the First Evangelical Free Church of Fullerton, California, since 1971. Chuck's radio program, "Insight for Living," began in 1979. In addition to his church and radio ministries, Chuck enjoys writing. He has authored numerous books and booklets on a variety of subjects.

Based on the outlines and transcripts of Chuck's sermons, the study guide text is co-authored by Lee Hough, a graduate of the University of Texas at Arlington and Dallas Theological Seminary. He also wrote the Living Insights sections.

Editor in Chief: Cynthia Swindoll	**Production Artists:** Gary Lett and Diana Vasquez
Coauthor of Text: Lee Hough	**Typographer:** Bob Haskins
Assistant Editor: Wendy Peterson	**Director, Communications Division:** Carla Beck
Copyediting Supervisor: Marty Anderson	**Project Manager:** Alene Cooper
Copy Editor: Marty Anderson	**Print Production Manager:** Deedee Snyder
Art Director: Steven Mitchell	**Assistant Production Manager:** John Norton
Designer: Gary Lett	**Printer:** Frye and Smith

Unless otherwise identified, all Scripture references are from the New American Standard Bible, © The Lockman Foundation 1960, 1962, 1963, 1968, 1971, 1972, 1973, 1975, 1977. Used by permission.

Other Scripture translations cited are The Amplified Bible (AMPLIFIED) and the King James Version (KJV).

© 1990 Charles R. Swindoll. All rights reserved.

Previous guides:
    © 1980, 1983 Charles R. Swindoll. All rights reserved.

Outlines and transcripts:
    © 1974 Charles R. Swindoll. All rights reserved.

An effort has been made to locate sources and obtain permission where necessary for the quotations used in this book. In the event of any unintentional omission, a modification will gladly be incorporated in future printings.

Notice

No portion of this publication may be translated into any language or reproduced in any form, except for brief quotations in reviews, without prior written permission of the publisher, Insight for Living, Post Office Box 4444, Fullerton, California 92634.

ISBN 0-8499-8417-3

Printed in the United States of America.

COVER PHOTOGRAPH: Rudi Weislein.

CONTENTS

1 Place to Begin . . . Discipleship   1
   John 1:35–48; Luke 9:18, 23

2 Question to Answer . . . Is Discipleship Biblical? . . .   10
   Matthew 28:19–20; 2 Timothy 2:2;
   Acts 9, 11, 13–18

3 Beginning of Discipleship . . . Selection   18
   Matthew 4:18–22; Luke 6:12–16;
   John 1:35–40; 6:66–68

4 Curriculum of Discipleship . . . Association   27
   Selected Scripture

5 Cost of Discipleship . . . Consecration   35
   Luke 14:25–35

6 Stimulus of Discipleship . . . Impartation   44
   John 13:33 14:6, Mark 6:31–52, Luke 11:1–4

7 Badge of Discipleship . . . Affection   54
   John 13:1–35

8 Genius of Discipleship . . . Delegation   64
   Exodus 18:13–27; Matthew 9:35–10:19, 17:14–20

9 Support of Discipleship . . . Intercession   74
   John 17:6–19

10 Advantage of Discipleship . . . Evaluation   82
    Selected Scripture

11 Goal of Discipleship . . . Reproduction   91
    Selected Scripture

12 Process of Discipleship . . . Demonstration   98
    2 Timothy 2:1–10

Books for Probing Further 107

Ordering Information/Order Form 111

INTRODUCTION

Years ago ministry was something most Christians watched happen. The minister carried out his work at a distance, preached from an elevated pulpit, and operated fairly aloof from his parishioners. Worshipers regularly attended a church service, sang the hymns, listened to a sermon, and unless they struggled with a particular problem requiring the pastor's time and attention, seldom got involved in ministry on a personal basis.

No longer.

The current emphasis is altogether different. Many Christians are now very much engaged in the work of ministry. We see ourselves as gifted members of the body of Christ, called to touch each others' lives and stimulate mutual growth. This is commonly referred to as *discipleship*, a term used to describe the process of building up one another in the faith. When kept in proper balance, it can be extremely effective in helping others grow toward maturity.

Several years ago I did an in-depth scriptural study of how Jesus trained His twelve. These messages are the result of my research. I should mention how grateful I am to Dr. Robert Coleman for his fine little book *Master Plan of Evangelism*, from which I have derived numerous ideas and illustrative points. It is must reading for all who desire to be engaged in an up-close-and-personal ministry with others.

And now . . . let's dig into this vital and exciting subject.

Chuck Swindoll

Chuck Swindoll

PUTTING TRUTH
INTO ACTION

Knowledge apart from application falls short of God's desire for His children. He wants us to apply what we learn so that we will change and grow. This study guide was prepared with these goals in mind. As you go through the following pages, we hope your desire to discover biblical truth will grow as your understanding of God's Word increases, and that you will be encouraged to apply what you've learned.

To assist you in your study, we've included a section called Living Insights at the end of each lesson. These exercises will challenge you to study further and to think of specific ways to put your discoveries into action.

There are many ways to use this guide—in personal devotions, group studies, discussions with friends and family, and Sunday school classes. And, of course, it's an ideal study aid when you're listening to its corresponding "Insight for Living" radio series.

To benefit most from this study guide, we would encourage you to consider it a spiritual journal. That's why we've included space in the Living Insights for recording your thoughts and discoveries. We hope you'll return to those sections often for review and encouragement as you continue to grow in your walk with Christ.

Lee Hough
Coauthor of Text
Author of Living Insights

Discipleship

MINISTRY UP CLOSE AND PERSONAL

Chapter 1

PLACE TO BEGIN...
DISCIPLESHIP

John 1:35–48; Luke 9:18, 23

When you were little, who did you dream of being when you grew up? A TV celebrity . . . Miss America . . . one of the cartoon superheroes? One minute you were just plain ol' you with droopy socks, and the next, you were a valiant warrior off in space fighting mutant woobies.

This series is about growing up to be like someone—not like a childhood hero, but like Christ. As God's children, we all have that opportunity, but not everyone takes it. As William Barclay writes,

> It is possible to be a follower of Jesus without being a disciple; to be a camp-follower without being a soldier of the king; to be a hanger-on in some great work without pulling one's weight. Once someone was talking to a great scholar about a younger man. He said, "So and so tells me that he was one of your students." The teacher answered devastatingly, "He may have attended my lectures, but he was not one of my students." There is a world of difference between attending lectures and being a student. It is one of the supreme handicaps of the Church that in the Church there are so many distant followers of Jesus and so few real disciples.[1]

---

1. William Barclay, *The Gospel of Luke,* 2d ed., The Daily Study Bible Series (Philadelphia, Pa.: The Westminster Press, 1956), p. 203.

1

Who do you want to grow up to be like? Whether you're seven or sixty-seven, it's never too late to start becoming like the Savior. The biggest adventure of our lives will start the day we commit with childlike abandon to being one of His disciples.

Essentials of Christianity

The goal of our study today is to explain what it means to be a disciple—not merely a Christian. But first, let's briefly review the tenets of Christianity on which true discipleship rests.

The founder of Christianity is the living, resurrected Lord, Jesus Christ. His goal is the salvation of individuals by the regeneration of their hearts through faith. And His method for spreading the Good News of salvation is not through political, educational, or even religious philosophies, but through disciples.

Essentials of Discipleship

Now let's turn our attention to Luke 9:23 for a look at the key character traits of a disciple.

> And He was saying to them all, "If anyone wishes to come after Me, let him deny himself, and take up his cross daily, and follow Me."

Backing up a little, we find out from verse 18 that the word *them* refers to the disciples. The words *all* and *anyone* tell us that no one is to be excluded. We can see, too, that Jesus is not offering salvation. Except for Judas, all those listening were already saved. Instead, Jesus is encouraging believers to become committed, devoted followers.

Notice also the words *wishes* and *let him.* They indicate that Christ is asking for a decision to become His disciple by following Him. Looking closer, we can discover three essential characteristics of a disciple.

First: *A disciple must "deny himself."* In Greek, the term *deny* means "to say no to something" and, in some instances, "to refuse someone." For example, Jesus used this word when He told Peter that he would soon deny knowing Him (John 13:38). The author of Hebrews also used it to describe Moses' refusal to be called the son of Pharaoh's daughter (Heb. 11:24). William Barclay defines it for us further.

Ordinarily we use the word *self-denial* in a restricted sense. We use it to mean doing without something, giving up something. For instance, a week of self-denial is a week when we do without certain pleasures or luxuries, usually in order to contribute to some good cause. But that is only a very small part of what Jesus meant by self-denial. To deny oneself means in every moment of life to say no to self, and to say yes to God. To deny oneself means once, finally and for all to dethrone self and to enthrone God. To deny oneself means to obliterate self as the dominant principle of life, and to make God the ruling principle, more, the ruling passion, of life. The life of constant self-denial is the life of constant assent to God.[2]

Second: *A disciple must "take up his cross daily."* A cross would have been a familiar sight to Jesus' followers—it wasn't uncommon to see a person dragging a crossbeam through the streets of Jerusalem toward the Place of the Skull. They all would have known that the cross was a symbol of death and that Jesus was asking them to daily put to death their own selfish desires and wills and to live only to accomplish His will.

Third: *A disciple must "follow Me."* At the heart of these two words is the idea of obedience. The Amplified Bible captures the thought best:

> . . . follow Me [cleave steadfastly to Me, conform wholly to My example, in living and if need be in dying also]. (Luke 9:23b)

Jesus' Method of Selecting Disciples

One of Jesus' challenges while He lived on earth was to establish a group of followers who would carry on His mission after He was gone. Let's look in the gospel of John to discover Jesus' approach to choosing those important people.

Jesus' Approach Was Personal

> Again the next day John was standing with two of his disciples, and he looked upon Jesus as He walked,

---

2. William Barclay, *The Gospel of Matthew*, vol. 2, 2d ed., The Daily Study Bible Series (Philadelphia, Pa.: The Westminster Press, 1958), p. 167.

and said, "Behold, the Lamb of God!" And the two disciples heard him speak, and they followed Jesus. And Jesus turned, and beheld them following, and said to them, "What do you seek?" (John 1:35–38a)

Jesus didn't care what these men wore, where they came from, or how much of the Law they knew. He was interested in their motives for following Him.

Jesus' Approach Was Individual

One of the two who heard John speak, and followed Him, was Andrew, Simon Peter's brother. He found first his own brother Simon, and said to him, "We have found the Messiah." . . . He brought him to Jesus. Jesus looked at him, and said, "You are Simon the son of John; you shall be called Cephas" (which translated means Peter). (vv. 40–42)

When Jesus saw this rough-hewn fisherman standing before Him, He knew not only who he was but what he was going to become.

Jesus' Approach Involved Looking for Certain Character Qualities

Jesus saw Nathanael coming to Him, and said of him, "Behold, an Israelite indeed, in whom is no guile!" Nathanael said to Him, "How do You know me?" Jesus answered and said to him, "Before Philip called you, when you were under the fig tree, I saw you." (vv. 47–48)

All through the process of selecting His disciples, Jesus peered through the windows of their souls to see the potential for growth.

As you read further about Jesus selecting His disciples, several more things stand out. First, He concentrated on harvesting a few disciples, not a massive following. Second, He was never in a hurry; He remained calm and methodical. Third, He didn't rely on gimmicks to motivate people to follow Him—He wasn't interested in discipling those who would always need something spectacular to keep them going. And, finally, He didn't thrust them into public ministry prematurely. Instead, He drew them to Himself.

And He went up to the mountain and summoned those whom He Himself wanted, and they came to Him. And He appointed twelve, that they might be with Him, and that He might send them out to preach. (Mark 3:13–14)

In *The Master Plan of Evangelism,* Robert Coleman asks and answers a valid question about Jesus' approach.

> Why? Why did Jesus deliberately concentrate His life upon comparatively so few people? Had He not come to save the world? With the glowing announcement of John the Baptist ringing in the ears of multitudes, the Master easily could have had an immediate following of thousands if He wanted them. Why did He not then capitalize upon His opportunities to enlist a mighty army of believers to take the world by storm? Surely the Son of God could have adopted a more enticing program of mass recruitment. Is it not rather disappointing that one with all the powers of the universe at His command would live and die to save the world, yet in the end have only a few ragged disciples to show for His labors? . . .
>
> Jesus was a realist. He fully realized the fickleness of depraved human nature as well as the Satanic forces of this world amassed against humanity, and in this knowledge He based His evangelism on a plan that would meet the need. The multitudes of discordant and bewildered souls were potentially ready to follow Him, but Jesus individually could not possibly give them the personal care they needed. His only hope was to get men imbued with His life who would do it for Him. Hence, He concentrated Himself upon those who were to be the beginning of this leadership. Though He did what He could to help the multitudes, He had to devote Himself primarily to a few men, rather than the masses, in order that the masses could at last be saved. This was the genius of His strategy.[3]

Jesus chose a few men *with* whom He could build a relationship and *in* whom He could pour His life so that when He was gone they could turn the world upside down.

3. Robert E. Coleman, *The Master Plan of Evangelism,* 2d ed. (Old Tappan, N.J.: Fleming H. Revell Co., Power Books, 1964), pp. 31, 33.

A Distinction: Believers and Disciples

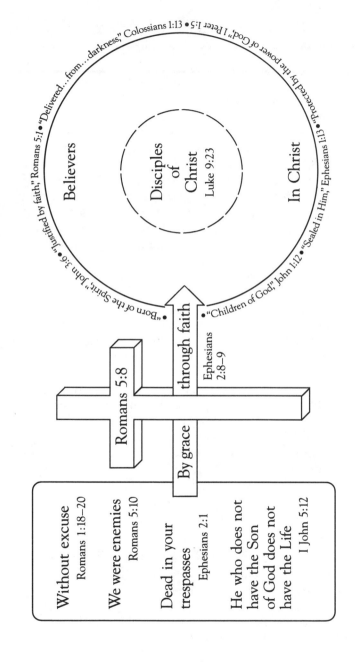

Believers

Disciples of Christ
Luke 9:23

In Christ

"Justified by faith," Romans 5:1 • "Delivered...from...darkness," Colossians 1:13 • "Protected by the power of God," I Peter 1:5

"Born of the Spirit," John 3:6

"Children of God," John 1:12 • "Sealed in Him," Ephesians 1:13

through faith

By grace

Romans 5:8

Ephesians 2:8–9

Without excuse
Romans 1:18–20

We were enemies
Romans 5:10

Dead in your trespasses
Ephesians 2:1

He who does not have the Son of God does not have the Life
I John 5:12

Copyright © 1974, 1990 Charles R. Swindoll. All rights reserved.

Discipleship Applied

As in any study, we can easily get caught up in gathering a lot of biblical data without ever really applying it to our lives. To avoid that, let's spend the next few moments evaluating our relationship with Christ. The diagram on the opposite page will help.

When we become Christians, we are automatically placed in the large circle, which represents the body of Christ. Within this circle, however, is a smaller one of committed disciples. God's desire is for the outer and inner circle to be one—for all believers to be His disciples.

As we conclude our study, won't you consider the following questions? They will help take discipleship off your mental bookshelf and put it into your life.

1. Are you a Christian? You cannot be one of Christ's disciples until you have entered into God's family through faith in His Son.

2. If you are a believer, which of the two circles are you in?

3. If you're not sure, ask yourself these questions:

    a. Do I really *want* to be a disciple?

    b. Am I willing to daily say no to self and yes to God's will— even if it means changing habits . . . or the whole course of my life?

4. Is there something keeping you from becoming Christ's disciple?

5. Would you like to start afresh, or possibly from scratch, having fellowship with Christ in that intimate circle of His disciples?

 Living Insights   STUDY ONE

Most of us remember playing follow-the-leader when we were little. But even as adults, we still play this game. The only difference is that our jumps and cartwheels have become more subtle and sophisticated. Following the leader may now mean driving a specific kind of a car, wearing certain clothes, or belonging to a particular church. Like lost sheep, we'll follow anyone who promises to meet our needs. For the disciple, however, there can be only one leader—Jesus.

• Did you answer the questions at the end of our lesson? Take time now to write down those responses.

1. Are you a Christian? Have you entered into God's family through faith in His Son Jesus?

_____

2. If you are a believer, which of the two circles are you in?

_____

3. If you're not sure, ask yourself,

   a. Do I really *want* to be a disciple? _____

   b. Am I willing to daily say no to self and yes to God's will— even if it means changing habits . . . or the whole course of my life?

   _____

4. If you're in the outer circle, is there something that is keeping you from becoming Christ's disciple? If so, what is it?

   _____

5. Would you like to start afresh, or possibly from scratch, having fellowship with Christ in that intimate circle reserved for His disciples?

   _____

6. Now answer one last question, Are you following Christ, or someone or something else?

   ☐ Christ   ☐ Someone else   ☐ Something else

🍇 *Living Insights* _____ STUDY TWO

Let's spend some time in prayer in response to this lesson and before we begin the rest of the series. To help get you started is a prayer from *Intimate Moments with the Savior* by Ken Gire, which

8

grows out of Christ's encounter with Zaccheus in Luke 19. The author has left off the traditional "Amen" so that you may continue in a prayer of your own.

Dear Jesus,

Forgive me for trying so long to compensate for my stunted growth. I have expected my work and my wealth to increase my stature. Help me to see, Lord, that an increase in my stature can only come as a result of a decrease in myself. It is in losing my life that I find it. It is in dying that I live. It is in giving that I receive.

I confess to you that I am short in spiritual stature. To even see you it seems that I'm always needing something to stand on.

But I want to see you. See you for who you really are. See you for myself, with my own two eyes. Not just through the eyes of a pastor. Or a teacher. Or an evangelist.

I've heard so much about you. How much is opinion? How much is hearsay? How much is truth? I want to know, for myself. I want to hear with my own ears. Not simply from a book. Or television. Or radio. Or a tape.

I'm tired of second-hand experience. I want to feel with my own heart.

If I have to climb a tree awkwardly and undignified to do so, I will gladly do it. Please come near, Lord. I'll be the one out on a limb, waiting.

And, as you come, overwhelm me with the awesome wonder that it is not I who seek you in the streets nearly as much as it is you who seeks me in the sycamores. . . .[4]

4. Ken Gire, *Intimate Moments with the Savior* (Grand Rapids, Mich.: Zondervan Publishing House, Daybreak Books, 1989), p. 78.

Chapter 2

QUESTION TO ANSWER . . . IS DISCIPLESHIP BIBLICAL?

Matthew 28:19–20; 2 Timothy 2:2; Acts 9, 11, 13–18

If asked whether discipleship is biblical, most of us would probably respond affirmatively without even giving it a second thought. Surely everybody with even a smattering of Bible background knows that—the same as they know that Noah gathered all the animals on the ark two by two, that money is the root of all evil, and that three kings worshiped the baby Jesus as He lay in a manger. Pretty basic stuff—right?

Wrong. Surprisingly, none of those last three "facts" are true. According to Genesis 7:1–3, Noah was to gather the clean animals into the ark by sevens and only the unclean animals by twos. In 1 Timothy 6:9–10, Paul says that it is the *love* of money that is the root of all sorts of evil, not money itself. And nowhere in Scripture does it say that three kings visited Joseph and Mary—it was wise men who came, and we're never told how many there were. Also, Matthew 2:11 says that when these wise men arrived, Joseph and his family were already living in a house, so Jesus would not have been a newborn lying in a manger as traditionally depicted.

Instead of these being common biblical truths, they're common biblical misconceptions. Could discipleship be another—something that sounds spiritual but isn't really biblical after all?

Suppose someone asked you for some hard biblical evidence to support discipleship. What would you say? For many of us, the strongest response we could muster would be, "Well, er, I know it's in the Bible someplace" or "My pastor preached on it once."

If those sound like answers you'd have to give, perhaps you would be interested in the case being tried in the courtroom of this lesson. Follow the proceedings carefully, as we examine the biblical evidence for discipleship.

Testimonies That Support Discipleship

To begin, we'll summon three witnesses from the New Testament whose divinely inspired testimonies endorse discipleship.

The first witness to take the stand is Jesus. It was the Lord Himself who established the biblical precedent of discipleship—not only by the example of His life, but also by these words to the disciples.

> "Go therefore and make disciples of all the nations, baptizing them in the name of the Father and the Son and the Holy Spirit, teaching them to observe all that I commanded you; and lo, I am with you always, even to the end of the age." (Matt. 28:19–20)

Jesus gave a crucial command in these two verses—"make disciples." He meant for the impact of His life and death to ripple outward in an ever-widening circle, through His disciples teaching others, who would then teach others, who would then teach others . . .

"Objection!" The prosecution protests, "Jesus' command to make disciples applied only to those eleven disciples to whom He was speaking, not to us today."

But here to offer irrefutable evidence to the contrary is our second witness—Dr. Luke. Writing about Paul and Barnabas, neither of whom were part of that original group, Luke tells us:

> And the next day [Paul] went away with Barnabas to Derbe. And after they had preached the gospel to that city and had made many disciples, they returned to Lystra and to Iconium and to Antioch. (Acts 14:20b–21)

Luke even uses the same term that Jesus used, *make disciples*, to describe Paul and Barnabas' work.

The final witness to take the stand on discipleship's behalf is the apostle Paul. Tucked away in his second letter to Timothy is perhaps the most familiar verse in all the New Testament on discipleship.

> The things which you have heard from me in the presence of many witnesses, these entrust to faithful men, who will be able to teach others also. (2 Tim. 2:2)

The word Paul uses here for *entrust* is a financial term; it means "to set something aside that is valuable." In this particular context, Paul charges Timothy to deposit the sound doctrine given to him into other men willing to follow Christ.

Exhibit A, on the following page, illustrates the flow of discipleship Paul described in 2 Timothy 2:2.

The Flow of Discipleship

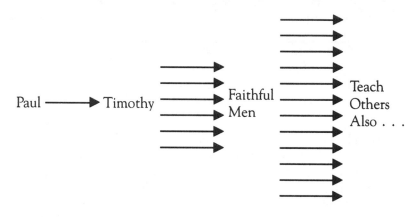

Paul discipled Timothy, depositing important spiritual truths into his life. Timothy, in turn, was to disciple other faithful men by depositing those same truths into their lives. And those men would then become disciplers in a multiplying return on Paul's initial deposit in Timothy's life.

An Example That Illustrates Discipleship

To see more clearly how discipleship works, let's briefly trace the lineage of disciplers and disciples in one man's spiritual heritage —Saul of Tarsus.

Background

Before his conversion, the apostle Paul was known as Saul of Tarsus. He was a brilliant Pharisee who was widely feared by the early church because of his hostile and aggressive persecution of Christians. According to Acts 9:1, Saul was "still breathing threats and murder against the disciples of the Lord" when suddenly he was saved (see vv. 1–18). Three days later, Saul the persecutor was being called Brother Saul by the very disciples in Damascus he had come to arrest. Everywhere in that city people were baffled by Paul's astonishing conversion.

> Now for several days he was with the disciples
> who were at Damascus, and immediately he began to

proclaim Jesus in the synagogues, saying, "He is the Son of God." And all those hearing him continued to be amazed, and were saying, "Is this not he who in Jerusalem destroyed those who called on this name, and who had come here for the purpose of bringing them bound before the chief priests?" (vv. 19b–21)

Paul later left Damascus when it was discovered that the Jews there were plotting to put him to death (see vv. 22–25). Returning to his home in Jerusalem, he immediately tried to join up with the Christians there.

And when he had come to Jerusalem, he was trying to associate with the disciples; and they were all afraid of him, not believing that he was a disciple. (v. 26)

The thought of Saul the Pharisee suddenly wanting to fellowship with believers was incredible to those persecuted Christians. The only Saul they knew was a killer with a maniacal lust for purging Israel of Christianity.

Contact

Paul's ostracism from the Christians in Jerusalem was short-lived, however—thanks to the help of one open-minded man.

But Barnabas took hold of [Paul] and brought him to the apostles and described to them how he had seen the Lord on the road, and that He had talked to him, and how at Damascus he had spoken out boldly in the name of Jesus. And he was with them moving about freely in Jerusalem, speaking out boldly in the name of the Lord. (vv. 27–28)

However, the betrayed Jews again plotted to kill the new convert, so he was sent by the disciples to the city of Tarsus (see vv. 29–30).

Sometime later the Jerusalem church sent Barnabas to Antioch, where enormous numbers of Gentiles were being converted (see 11:19–24). But the needs for discipleship were too great for one person to handle. So Barnabas

left for Tarsus to look for Saul; and when he had found him, he brought him to Antioch. And it came about that for an entire year they met with the church, and taught considerable numbers; and the disciples were first called Christians in Antioch. (vv. 25–26)

During this time Barnabas discipled Paul and also gave him the vision for discipling others.

Process

Now let's watch Paul move into the role of discipler.

After ministering in Antioch, Paul and Barnabas traveled together on an extended missionary journey (see chaps. 13–14), on which the two of them made many disciples (14:21). Beginning in Acts 18, however, we see Paul reaching out to disciple on his own.

After these things he left Athens and went to Corinth. And he found a certain Jew named Aquila, a native of Pontus, having recently come from Italy with his wife Priscilla, because Claudius had commanded all the Jews to leave Rome. He came to them, and because he was of the same trade, he stayed with them and they were working; for by trade they were tentmakers. (vv. 1–3)

This was Paul's first time to set foot in Corinth, and no doubt it was comforting to find two other newcomers to live and work with. But there was much more than companionship going on—for the next year and a half, Paul modeled for this husband and wife the characteristics of a disciple. When it came time for Paul to set sail for Syria, he took Aquila and Priscilla with him as far as Ephesus (vv. 18–19). There he left his two disciples to begin their own ministry.

Aquila and Priscilla had settled down in Ephesus to make tents and disciples, when one day a Jew named Apollos came to Ephesus and began teaching about Christ (vv. 24–25). Immediately they detected holes in his theology and helped by supplying a few patches.

When Priscilla and Aquila heard him, they took him aside and explained to him the way of God more accurately. (v. 26b)

For an unrevealed period of time afterward, Apollos benefited from the discipling ministry of Paul through Aquila and Priscilla.

Later, Apollos traveled to Achaia, in Greece, to disciple believers there. Ironically, part of the time that Apollos was in Greece, he stayed in Corinth (Acts 18:27–19:1), watering the very seeds of discipleship that had been planted by Paul (see 18:1–17)!

Benefits That Stem from Discipleship

Hopefully, by now you've seen enough evidence to be convinced that discipleship is biblical. So instead of offering more proof, we'd like to present you with some of the benefits of discipleship.

Discipleship reinforces the ministry of the Word by personalizing it. In the discipleship process, the ones being discipled have the written Word fleshed out for them in the life of the discipler. Barnabas personalized the Word for Paul, who modeled it for Aquila and Priscilla, who in turn demonstrated it for Apollos.

Discipleship translates biblical truth into practical living. For many people, Christianity is nothing more than a sterile intellectualism; Sunday after Sunday, they simply add another sermon to their collection without ever applying it to their lives. Discipleship means having help in taking the Scriptures from your head to your heart.

Discipleship develops character qualities in the lives of Christians. A Christlike character doesn't come from sitting in a pew but from growing through personal circumstances. Effective discipleship involves explaining God's Word and how it relates to our daily lives.

Discipleship is not limited. The process of discipleship is not limited to Sunday mornings or stained-glass church buildings. It can occur at any time, in any place, and at any age.

Discipleship is not structured. Discipleship doesn't mean singing three hymns, praying, and then having a sermon. Instead, it's a way of life, like Jesus'—something that could never be captured in outline form on a sheet of paper.

Discipleship is not a program. In the Scriptures, the process of discipleship always takes place in the context of relationships. True discipleship can be transmitted no other way. *Programs* tend to turn out Christians committed to being entertained. *Discipleship* trains up Christians committed to loving and obeying the Lord Jesus.

At the beginning of this lesson we raised the question, Is discipleship biblical? We have found that it's not only biblical but beneficial. And we can even go a step further—it's not only beneficial, it's essential. How essential it is to your own life, we will explore in a more practical way in the Living Insights.

People hunger to see the reality of Christ—to have God's Word explained by a living example rather than by a set of notes. Commonly attributed to St. Francis of Assisi is the admonition

Preach Jesus, and only when necessary use words.

How long has it been since someone discipled you with their life and not just their words? How long has it been since you've done that for someone else?

- Is there a mature Christian in your church whom you could approach about discipling you? If so, who?

_____

- Is there someone in your church, at work, or possibly in your neighborhood whom you could begin discipling?

_____

Let's go back to our courtroom scenario for a moment.

"Has the jury reached a verdict?"
"Yes, your honor. We the jury find the defendant—biblical."
"Court's adjourned."
"Excuse me."
"Yes?"
"I'm a reporter with the *Discipleship Daily News*. I wonder if I could ask you a couple of questions before you leave?"
"Sure."
"Do you agree with the jury's finding that discipleship is biblical?"
"You bet. And there's plenty of evidence. For instance—"
"That's OK, I've already got all of that here in my notes. What I would like to know is this: Since you agree that discipleship is biblical, when and who can the people expect you to start discipling?"
"Well, I, uh, I'm no Paul, of course. What I mean is . . ."
"You did say you believed discipleship is biblical?"
"Well, yes. However . . . "

For many of us, this fictitious conversation would hit pretty close to home if we were the one being questioned. Intellectually, we agree that discipleship is biblical. However . . . in our hearts, the thought of actually discipling someone scares us to death.

But once we get those fears out in the open, maybe we'll find they aren't as big and scary as we thought. Maybe we *can* begin discipling others.

- For the next few minutes, try to identify some of those fears that keep you from this important task.

_____

_____

_____

_____

- Now take a second look at those fears. Are they based on truth? Is there something you can do to overcome them?

_____

_____

_____

_____

Chapter 3

BEGINNING OF DISCIPLESHIP... SELECTION

Matthew 4:18–22; Luke 6:12–16; John 1:35–40, 6:66–68

Have you ever noticed what goes on in the produce section of your local grocery store? For years now, people who frequent the fruits and vegetables have been perfecting the fine art of selection. So what? Well, for starters, so they can detect a mouth-watering watermelon with a thump, sniff out the exact day to make a fruit salad out of a pineapple, or read the inside of an avocado with a squeeze.

Now before you pooh-pooh any of this, think about how *you* make selections. Coin tosses? Eeny-meeny-miny-moe? Picking a name out of a hat? That's Dark Ages stuff! Sure, drawing straws and paper-scissors-rock are fun, but they can hardly compare with thumping, sniffing, and squeezing. And the produce technique isn't limited to just what goes in your refrigerator. Haven't you ever seen someone thump the tires on a new car? Why, it can make the difference between buying a real cream puff or being stuck with a lemon—or so some believe.

Seriously, we all have our ways of thumping, sniffing, and squeezing to help us choose. But what's the best technique when it comes to choosing disciples? Squeezing tomatoes is OK, but that's hardly what you want to do to find someone to disciple.

Today we want to focus on the first major step of discipleship—selection—based on Jesus' example. What sort of thumping, sniffing, and squeezing did He do? What were the choice qualities He looked for in a disciple?

Jesus' Technique of Selection

Before Jesus' notoriety reached its peak, He handpicked twelve men to be His disciples. Why? Because Jesus wasn't concerned "with programs to reach the multitudes, but with men whom the multitudes would follow."[1]

---

1. Robert E. Coleman, *The Master Plan of Evangelism*, 2d ed. (Old Tappan, N.J.: Fleming H. Revell Co., Power Books, 1964), p. 21.

The word *disciple* comes from the Greek root for *mathētēs*, meaning "to learn, to receive instruction." Jesus' disciples were to be learners of Him.

Before the Selection

In preparation for the selection of His disciples, Jesus first got away from the crowds to be alone with God,

> and it was at this time that He went off to the mountain to pray, and He spent the whole night in prayer to God. (Luke 6:12)

Once secluded in his mountain aerie, Jesus prayed His way through the night, talking with His Father about the twelve He would pick on the morrow.

The Selection Itself

Jesus had already attracted many followers, but only a handful were chosen as disciples.

> And when day came, He called His disciples to Him; and chose twelve of them, whom He also named as apostles. (v. 13)

Mark 3:14 says that Jesus called the disciples to be "with Him," not to follow a set of notes in some classroom. They were to become Jesus' closest companions, the living books upon which He would imprint His message to the rest of the world.[2]

Back in Luke 6:13, we see that Jesus immediately bestowed on His newly selected disciples the added title of apostles. The word *apostle* in Greek conveyed to those men the idea of "being sent forth as a messenger." Quite possibly, it was at this moment that Jesus first communicated something of His plan to train them as disciples and then send them forth in His name as apostles.

---

2. Jesus' disciples are listed four times in the New Testament: Matthew 10:2–4, Mark 3:16–19, Luke 6:14–16, and Acts 1:13. The names are not listed in the same order in these passages, and it is also helpful to know that Thaddaeus and Judas (the son of James) are one and the same. This also applies to Bartholomew and Nathanael (mentioned in John 1:45) and Simon the Cananaean and Simon the Zealot. The reason for these discrepancies is easily explained by the fact that some of the lists use their given names while others use their formal names.

The Basis of Selection

Before we examine why Jesus chose those twelve men listed in Luke 6:14–16, let's learn a little more about them from Robert Coleman's *The Master Plan of Evangelism.*

> What is more revealing about these men is that at first they do not impress us as being key men. None of them occupied prominent places in the Synagogue, nor did any of them belong to the Levitical priesthood. For the most part they were common laboring men, probably having no professional training beyond the rudiments of knowledge necessary for their vocation. Perhaps a few of them came from families of some considerable means, such as the sons of Zebedee, but none of them could have been considered wealthy. They had no academic degrees in the arts and philosophies of their day. Like their Master, their formal education likely consisted only of the Synagogue schools. Most of them were raised in the poor section of the country around Galilee. Apparently the only one of the twelve who came from the more refined region of Judea was Judas Iscariot. By any standard of sophisticated culture then and now they would surely be considered as a rather ragged aggregation of souls. One might wonder how Jesus could ever use them. They were impulsive, temperamental, easily offended, and had all the prejudices of their environment. . . . Not the kind of group one would expect to win the world for Christ.[3]

If it wasn't education, culture, or status, what were the qualities Jesus was looking for? Through a brief study in the Gospels, we can glean at least four prominent characteristics shared by Jesus' fledgling learners.

They Were Available

Aside from their spiritual desire, the first noticeable quality about these men was their availability.

3. Coleman, *Master Plan of Evangelism*, pp. 22–23.

Take Peter and Andrew, for example. As fishermen, their whole lives were barnacled to the routine of catching and selling fish. And yet when Christ called them, they were willing to break loose and follow Him.

> And walking by the Sea of Galilee, He saw two brothers, Simon who was called Peter, and Andrew his brother, casting a net into the sea; for they were fishermen. And He said to them, "Follow Me, and I will make you fishers of men." And they immediately left the nets, and followed Him. (Matt. 4:18–20)

The remarkable word in this account is *immediately*. Neither of the two brothers hesitated in laying down their nets, their former lives, so that they could take up following Jesus.

James and John, Peter and Andrew's fishing partners, were also quick to follow Christ's call.

> And going on from there He saw two other brothers, James the son of Zebedee, and John his brother, in the boat with Zebedee their father, mending their nets; and He called them. And they immediately left the boat and their father, and followed Him. (vv. 21–22)

Fishermen weren't the only ones, however, who were ready to follow Christ. In Luke 5:27–28, Jesus called a tax collector named Levi, better known as Matthew, who promptly walked out of a lucrative career to follow Christ.

> And after that He went out, and noticed a tax-gatherer named Levi, sitting in the tax office, and He said to him, "Follow Me." And he left everything behind, and rose and began to follow Him.

They Were Flexible

These men were fed up with the religious system of the Pharisees. For years it had buried their worship of God under a mountain of man-made laws. And because of that, they weren't afraid to listen to a voice crying in the wilderness—a voice like John the Baptist's.

John the Baptist was not your typical religious leader. The only synagogue he ever taught in was the wilderness. He preferred dressing in camel's hair instead of pious tasseled robes. And he disregarded the Pharisees' meticulous diet in favor of wild honey and locusts. But most of all, it was John's *message* that radically differed from the religious establishment's. John spoke of a coming Messiah, not of the Pharisees' latest tradition.

We know that at least one of Jesus' disciples had followed this austere messenger. And in heeding the voice of the one sent to prepare the way, this disciple soon found himself following the One who was the Way.

> Again the next day John was standing with two of his disciples, and he looked upon Jesus as He walked, and said, "Behold, the Lamb of God!" And the two disciples heard him speak, and they followed Jesus. . . . One of the two who heard John speak, and followed Him, was Andrew, Simon Peter's brother. (John 1:35–37, 40)

The flexibility exhibited by Andrew's willingness to go against the established religion was a quality shared by all the disciples who dared to follow Christ.

They Were Teachable

Almost without exception, the disciples were always open and teachable. They may not have always understood Jesus, but they at least possessed a willingness to learn.

They Were Dependable

At times, Jesus thinned the ranks of those following Him with words that were judged by His audience as being shocking, enigmatic, and impossible to follow. But even though many withdrew and criticized Jesus, these twelve disciples remained loyal in their commitment to follow Him.

> As a result of this many of His disciples withdrew, and were not walking with Him anymore. Jesus said therefore to the twelve, "You do not want to go away also, do you?" Simon Peter answered Him, "Lord, to whom shall we go? You have words of eternal life." (6:66–68)

Practical Suggestions for Today

So far our lesson has shown us One who wanted to disciple others and twelve who wanted to be discipled. Now let's move forward nineteen centuries and see how the principles from Jesus' model of discipleship can be applied today.

Those Wishing to Disciple Others

If you have been a growing Christian for some time and desire to have a discipleship ministry, begin first with a personal study of how Jesus trained His disciples. Don't expect, however, to master the Master's techniques in two weeks. Think more along the lines of a lifetime. Allow Jesus to teach you how to disciple by regularly spending time with Him and His disciples in the Gospels.

Second, commit to praying regularly about your desire to disciple. Ask God for His clear direction about the approach to take, the words to say. Pray about whom God would have you select— possibly someone you lead to the Lord, a neighbor, or someone in your Sunday school class. You might also ask God for sensitivity in discerning a person's needs beneath the surface mask. The important thing is to pray and take this first step of selection slowly, carefully . . . just as Jesus did (see Luke 6:12–13).

Third, remember to keep your group small and the selection process quiet. Discipleship isn't about big crowds and gaining lots of attention. In fact, as you study the Gospels you'll see that Jesus never publicized this part of His ministry. Discipling others is a personal ministry that requires a privacy and intimacy not found in limelight programs.

Fourth, after you have begun doing the three things mentioned above, plan to meet regularly with the person you're discipling. Consistency is the key for someone to be able to pick up the Christlike qualities you're wanting to impart, as you experience life together.

Those Wishing to be Discipled

For those of you wanting to be discipled, you first need to ask God for a discipler. Don't try to hurry the process by rushing out ahead of God and choosing someone yourself. Let Him make the selection.[4]

After you have spent time in prayer for this person, begin communicating your desire to be discipled to people you respect spiritually. Perhaps your pastor, an officer in the church, or a Bible study

---

4. A good example of letting God make the selection can be found in the way Paul's discipling ministry with Timothy started. Acts 16:1–3 records how God linked these two together and how Timothy immediately began being discipled by Paul.

companion. One of these people could connect you with or may be the person God has chosen to disciple you.

Last, remember to stay alert and sensitive to God's leading as you communicate with others about your desire.

A Concluding Thought

In Ephesians 4:11–12, Paul lays out God's blueprint for growth in His church. He tells us that the Lord has given gifted people to the body of Christ for the "equipping of the saints." Why? For a work of service that will ultimately build up the entire body of Christ.

The Greek word used here for *service* means "ministering to one another." It's a relational concept that necessitates the equipped saints getting involved in people's lives—not making a career out of sitting in a pew next to strangers each week. Are you serving the body of Christ? Could it be that God wants to shake you out of your comfortable routine to begin meeting the needs of His body by discipling others?

If you are serious about doing a work of service, then use that keen eye you have for picking out the basket with the most cherry tomatoes in it to start looking for someone to disciple, someone who is available . . . flexible . . . teachable . . . and dependable.

 Living Insights STUDY ONE

For Peter and Andrew, being flexible enough to follow Christ involved taking incredible risks.

Can you imagine what some of their fishing buddies might have said the day these two brothers laid down their nets to follow Christ?

"Simon! Andrew! Has the sun gone to your heads? It's taken years for you to build up your fishing business; don't throw it all away for some religious dreamer. Besides, what kind of leader is this who takes fishermen to be his holy men? Do you want to be known as fools, to become the laughingstock of Galilee? You'll ruin your lives. Be practical, think about your families, your future."

To follow Christ, the disciples all had to risk being misunderstood, maligned, and rejected.

- Beginning with the disciples and, then, moving into your own life, list some of the other risks that keep people from being flexible enough to follow Christ.

_____

_____

_____

_____

_____

_____

- Of all the things you listed, which is the most difficult for you to overcome? Why?

_____

_____

_____

_____

🍇 *Living Insights* STUDY TWO

Let's say you're ready to go out and begin looking for someone to disciple. How are you going to tell if someone is available, flexible, teachable, and dependable?

- Spend the next few minutes brainstorming some practical ways of discerning the four qualities of a disciple.

Available: _____

_____

_____

_____

Flexible: _____

_____

PROPERTY OF
BROADWAY CHRISTIAN CHURCH LIBRARY
910 BROADWAY
FORT WAYNE, IN 46802

Teachable: _____

_____

_____

_____

Dependable: _____

_____

_____

_____

Chapter 4

CURRICULUM OF DISCIPLESHIP... ASSOCIATION

Selected Scripture

When Jesus called His disciples, He called them first and foremost to be "with Him" (Mark 3:14). Read what Robert Coleman says about the relationship between Jesus and His men.

> They walked together along the lonely roads; they visited together in the crowded cities; they sailed and fished together in the Sea of Galilee; they prayed together in the deserts and in the mountains; and they worshipped together in the Synagogues and in the Temple.
>
> Such close and constant association, of course, meant virtually that Jesus had no time to call His own. Like little children clamoring for the attention of their father, the disciples were always under foot of the Master. . . . But Jesus would have it no other way. He wanted to be with them. They were His spiritual children . . . and the only way that a father can properly raise a family is to be with them.[1]

What Association Involved Then

Instead of raising disciples, many churches today foster latchkey Christians—spiritual children given the key to the door of the kingdom of God, but no discipler to help them grow up. As a result, pewfuls of Christians everywhere share the same stunted testimony of spiritual growth with this young boy from Argentina.

> "Within six months of my conversion I knew everything everybody else knew in the church. From that

---

1. Robert E. Coleman, *The Master Plan of Evangelism*, 2d ed. (Old Tappan, N.J.: Fleming H. Revell Co., Power Books, 1964), pp. 43–44.

27

six months on, I was just maintained in the congregation. I grew just so far and I stayed there."[2]

The latchkey method of training up Christians has left the church weak and immature. We need to get back to Jesus' curriculum of discipleship. And perhaps the best way to begin is by looking at what Jesus offered the disciples when He first called them—discipleship by association with Him.

Initial Encounter

When Jesus began gathering His disciples, the most common method of discipleship was the one practiced by the Pharisees. To be considered one of their followers, one had to abide by a punctilious system of 365 prohibitions and 250 commandments. Anyone who could not keep up with their meticulous version of the Mosaic Law was labeled a sinner. Jesus, on the other hand, had only one requirement—to follow Him.

> And as He was going along by the Sea of Galilee,
> He saw Simon and Andrew, the brother of Simon,
> casting a net in the sea; for they were fishermen.
> And Jesus said to them, "Follow Me, and I will make
> you become fishers of men." (Mark 1:16–17)

Jesus didn't offer His disciples a textbook to study. There weren't any membership classes to attend, notes to memorize, or rules and regulations to master. He "was His own school and curriculum."[3] And His disciples were enrolled the moment they laid down their nets to follow Him (see vv. 18–20 and John 1:43). This togetherness extended even into where Jesus was staying.

> Again the next day John was standing with two
> of his disciples, and he looked upon Jesus as He
> walked, and said, "Behold, the Lamb of God!" And
> the two disciples heard him speak, and they followed
> Jesus. And Jesus turned, and beheld them following,
> and said to them, "What do you seek?" And they said
> to Him, "Rabbi (which translated means Teacher),
> where are You staying?" He said to them, "Come, and

2. As quoted by Juan Carlos Ortiz and Jamie Buckingham in *Call to Discipleship* (Plainfield, N.J.: Logos International, 1975), p. 11.

3. Coleman, *The Master Plan of Evangelism*, p. 38.

you will see." They came therefore and saw where
He was staying; and they stayed with Him that day,
for it was about the tenth hour. (John 1:35–39)

By opening the door of the place where He was staying, Jesus
was opening the door to a relationship with Him. And that interaction was the key to his method of discipleship. The more you study
Jesus' ministry with His followers, the more clearly the pattern
emerges—He consistently chose being with His disciples over being
with the masses.[4]

The Training Period

Perhaps the passage that best describes Jesus' process of association is found in Matthew 11:28–29.

"Come to Me, all who are weary and heavy-laden,
and I will give you rest. Take My yoke upon you,
and learn from Me, for I am gentle and humble in
heart; and you shall find rest for your souls."

Tucked away in these verses are two phrases that summarize
discipleship—"come to Me" and "learn from Me." We've seen
Christ call the disciples to come to Him. Now let's examine how
the disciples learned from Him.

By having the disciples with Him, Jesus was able to weave whatever lessons needed to be taught into their everyday experiences.
One such occasion is recorded in Matthew 8. There Jesus held class
on board a sinking boat in the middle of a terrible storm. The subject covered was faith, and Jesus' pupils were very motivated to learn!

And when He got into the boat, His disciples
followed Him. And behold, there arose a great storm
in the sea, so that the boat was covered with waves;
but He Himself was asleep. And they came to Him,
and awoke Him, saying, "Save us, Lord; we are perishing!" And He said to them, "Why are you timid,
you men of little faith?" Then He arose, and rebuked
the winds and the sea; and it became perfectly calm.

---

4. Even in the few hours before His death, Jesus sought out His disciples (see John 13–17).
"Contrary to what one might expect, as the ministry of Christ lengthened into the second
and third years He gave increasingly more time to the chosen disciples, not less." Coleman,
The Master Plan of Evangelism, pp. 40–41.

And the men marveled, saying, "What kind of a man is this, that even the winds and the sea obey Him?" (vv. 23–27)

Jesus also found another classroom setting from which to teach his disciples—a mountainside blanketed with hungry people.

And Jesus went up on the mountain, and there He sat with His disciples. Now the Passover, the feast of the Jews, was at hand. Jesus therefore lifting up His eyes, and seeing that a great multitude was coming to Him, said to Philip, "Where are we to buy bread, that these may eat?" And this He was saying to test him; for He Himself knew what He was intending to do. (John 6:3–6)

Jesus could have easily caused manna to rain down from heaven to feed the people. Instead, He used the situation to present his student disciples with a pop quiz on faith and impossibilities.

Philip answered Him, "Two hundred denarii worth of bread is not sufficient for them, for everyone to receive a little." One of His disciples, Andrew, Simon Peter's brother, said to Him, "There is a lad here who has five barley loaves and two fish, but what are these for so many people?" (vv. 7–9)

Had Jesus been grading this exam, Philip, Andrew, and all the rest of the disciples who stood there scratching their heads would have flunked. Philip responded as if it was a quiz on finances, and Andrew thought it was a scavenger hunt to find enough people's lunches to share. But Jesus didn't scold His disciples for not getting the right answer. Instead, He patiently told everyone to take a seat and began a class on faith versus impossibilities that the disciples would never forget.

Jesus said, "Have the people sit down." Now there was much grass in the place. So the men sat down, in number about five thousand. Jesus therefore took the loaves; and having given thanks, He distributed to those who were seated; likewise also of the fish as much as they wanted. (vv. 10–11)

Even after the people had eaten their fill, Jesus still had one more exercise for the disciples.

And when they were filled, He said to His disciples, "Gather up the leftover fragments that nothing may be lost." And so they gathered them up, and filled twelve baskets with fragments from the five barley loaves, which were left over by those who had eaten. (vv. 12–13)

Jesus concluded His impromptu class with an object lesson. To each of the twelve disciples, those twelve baskets of leftovers planted a truth that Jesus wanted to take root in their minds: With God, nothing is impossible.

What Association Involves Today

We've seen from Jesus' example that we can't expect to disciple from a distance. We have to be willing to open up our lives, to be with our disciples on a regular basis, and to give them the close attention they need.

With that in mind, here are four insights to help prepare you for discipling others by association.

Association Has Threatening Moments

Mark Twain once said, "Everyone is a moon, and has a dark side which he never shows to anybody."[5] The threatening thing about discipling others is the fear of having our dark sides, our failures and weaknesses, exposed. We're afraid of what our disciples will think; we're afraid of rejection and exposure. And so we would rather teach a class from a set of notes than allow a disciple to take notes on the way we live.

Association Calls for Sacrifice

Discipling others means a sacrifice of time. It also means a sacrifice in schedule, skipping some enjoyable things in order to keep this relationship a priority. It also means the sacrifice of some privacy, opening home and heart to another person.

Association Requires Total Honesty

A facade can fool people from a distance. But in the closeness of a discipling relationship, no facade can hide the nicks and cracks

---

5. Mark Twain, in *Bartlett's Familiar Quotations*, 14th ed., rev. and enl., ed. Emily Morison Beck (Boston, Mass.: Little, Brown and Co., 1968), p. 763.

in our lives. Ironically, though, those weaknesses usually draw people to us rather than drive them away. They're what make us seem real.

Association Is a Test of Love and Loyalty

The real test of loving someone comes when we no longer stand back and simply tell them what to do, but when we get down in the trenches with them and lend a hand. As Jesus said, "Greater love has no one than this, that one lay down his life for his friends" (John 15:13). Discipleship is not simply describing the Christian life, it's demonstrating it by voluntarily laying down your life for another.

In every discipleship ministry there are private thoughts shared that should never be mentioned outside that relationship. And it is in the faithful keeping of these vulnerable thoughts that we prove ourselves to be loyal and worthy to be trusted.

A Final Thought

The tragedy today, of course, is that few Christian schools or churches emphasize discipleship. And yet this was at the heart of Jesus' ministry. Robert Coleman asks,

> When will the church learn this lesson? . . .
>
> . . . Most churches insist on bringing new members through some kind of a confirmation class which usually meets an hour a week for a month or so. But the rest of the time the young convert has no contact at all with a definite Christian training program, except as he may attend the worship services of the church and the Sunday School.
>
> . . . If Sunday services and membership training classes are all that a church has to develop young converts into mature disciples, then they are defeating their own purpose. . . . There is simply no substitute for getting with people, and it is ridiculous to imagine that anything less, short of a miracle, can develop strong Christian leadership. After all, if Jesus, the Son of God, found it necessary to stay almost constantly with His few disciples for three years, and even one of them was lost, how can a church expect to do this job on an assembly line basis a few days out of the year?[6]

6. Coleman, *The Master Plan of Evangelism*, pp. 47–48.

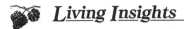
You may be wondering how you're going to find the time to disciple someone by association. It's a demanding commitment, and your schedule is already pretty packed.

But before you give up hope, try applying this simple principle:

Never go anywhere alone.

Like a metal detector, this principle can help you unearth some golden opportunities for discipling that lay buried in your schedule. For example, below is a list of things we often do that are potentially good discipleship times.

Shopping at the mall	Celebrating a holiday
Going to a show	Exercising

- For the next few minutes, go over your schedule with this principle in mind. As you discover opportunities for getting together with a disciple, write them down and start using them!

_____

_____

_____

_____

_____

_____

 Living Insights   STUDY TWO

It seems that the only place and time many Christians hear God's Word is in a pew on Sunday mornings. Jesus' disciples, on the other hand, were taught in a boat, on a mountainside, and along the roads of Palestine. They learned from a blind man being healed that Jesus was the light. They saw the importance of faith when Peter walked on water. And they grasped Christ's principle of humility in leadership when He washed their feet.

Notebooks, diagrams, and overhead projectors are great for classrooms, but they're not always that practical when you're out and about with your disciple.

- Take some time now to brainstorm ways you can weave lessons from God's Word into day-to-day experiences—for example, discussing popular movies and the values they portray or pointing out God's attributes as they're displayed in nature.

_____

_____

_____

_____

_____

_____

_____

_____

_____

_____

_____

Chapter 5

COST OF DISCIPLESHIP...
CONSECRATION
Luke 14:25–35

Every time you consider the cost of discipleship, you can count on one thing: your sin nature is going to haggle with your new nature over the price. The flesh will whine that Christ's demands are too painful; it will grouse that you have to give up too much; and it will fuss that you're being cheated. The bottom line of all these wranglings, of course, is to keep the cost to a minimum, to arrive at a comfortable price.

> I would like to buy $3 worth of God, please, not enough to explode my soul or disturb my sleep, but just enough to equal a cup of warm milk or a snooze in the sunshine. I don't want enough of Him to make me . . . pick beets with a migrant. I want ecstasy, not transformation; I want the warmth of the womb, not a new birth. I want a pound of the Eternal in a paper sack. I would like to buy $3 worth of God, please.[1]

Shallow and superficial Christianity can always be bought for the price of a little loose-change commitment—but discipleship cannot. In our lesson today we will be studying the cost of gaining the right to be called Christ's disciples, based on the price tag found in Luke 14:25–33.

The Setting

> Now great multitudes were going along with Him.
> (v. 25a)

Like bees to honey, Jesus' public ministry attracted a following so thick He could hardly brush the people away long enough to catch His breath.

---

1. Wilbur Rees, "$3.00 Worth of God," as quoted by Tim Hansel in *When I Relax I Feel Guilty* (Elgin, Ill.: David C. Cook Publishing Co., 1979), p. 49.

And in this great potpourri of followers mingled interested seekers, skeptics who didn't buy any of what Jesus said, and a large number of window shoppers. People who simply enjoyed looking, listening, and occasionally getting free food.

The Terms of Consecration

It was to this crowd of seekers, skeptics, and the "just looking" that Jesus turned and quoted the stringent costs for being one of His disciples. Three times Christ thinned the ranks of those following Him with three exacting terms for consecration. Each requirement brandished the sobering thought that unless they were willing to do as He said, they could not be His disciple. Let's find out what those terms were—and still are.

Personal Relationships

"If anyone comes to Me, and does not hate his own father and mother and wife and children and brothers and sisters, yes, and even his own life, he cannot be My disciple." (v. 26)

In *The Bible Knowledge Commentary*, John Martin unlocks the meaning behind Jesus' enigmatic imagery.

Literally hating one's family would have been a violation of the Law. Since Jesus on several occasions admonished others to fulfill the Law, He must not have meant here that one should literally hate his family. The stress here is on the priority of love (cf. Matt. 10:37). One's loyalty to Jesus must come before his loyalty to his family or even to life itself. Indeed, those who did follow Jesus against their families' desires were probably thought of as hating their families.[2]

No doubt this was too high a price for many, so they began to leave. But Jesus didn't reduce the cost of discipleship to lure them back. Instead, He raised it with the next term, which called for an even deeper commitment to consecration.

---

2. John A. Martin, "Luke," in *The Bible Knowledge Commentary*, New Testament ed., ed. John F. Walvoord and Roy B. Zuck (Wheaton, Ill.: SP Publications, Victor Books, 1983), p. 243.

Personal Goals and Desires

> "Whoever does not carry his own cross and come after Me cannot be My disciple." (v. 27)

Here Jesus invoked an explicit image that was familiar to everyone in the crowd. The cross was a symbol of death, a violent death shrouded in shame. Jesus was saying that to be His disciple meant to put to death self, that pride or self-centeredness in all of us that rebels against God. In Romans 12:1, the apostle Paul exhorts the saints in Rome to continue putting the self to death, in order to be Christ's disciples.

> I urge you therefore, brethren, by the mercies of God, to present your bodies a living and holy sacrifice, acceptable to God, which is your spiritual service of worship.

Later, in the same letter to the Romans, Paul fleshes out this term for discipleship in a practical way that his readers would understand.

> Now we who are strong ought to bear the weaknesses of those without strength and not just please ourselves. Let each of us please his neighbor for his good, to his edification.[3] (15:1–2)

All of us must choose whether to live according to God's desires or continue wandering, as Isaiah describes, "All of us like sheep have gone astray, Each of us has turned to his own way" (Isa. 53:6a).

To see whether you're living according to your own desires and goals or God's, ask yourself three questions:

First: Have you honestly and objectively taken your life's goals before the Lord for His approval?

Second: Do your goals feed your ego more than they honor the Lord?

And third: Are you really willing to change your goals if God were to show you that you should?

Remember, "Self cannot and will not follow Him, but taking up one's cross results in death to self and newness of life in Christ Jesus."[4]

---

3. For further study, see Philippians 2:3–4.

4. Miles J. Stanford, *Principles of Spiritual Growth* (Lincoln, Nebr.: Back to the Bible, 1977), p. 74.

Personal Possessions

> "So therefore, no one of you can be My disciple who does not give up all his own possessions." (Luke 14:33)

Again, Jesus was not speaking in literal terms. He's not saying that His disciples aren't supposed to own anything, rather, that no possession is supposed to own a disciple. People often become slaves to the material things they buy, whether homes, cars, or even clothes. These things are not wrong in themselves, it's only when they keep us from being freed up to follow Him that they infringe on Christ's rightful ownership of our lives. In a personal conversation, Corrie ten Boom said,

> "Chuck, I've learned that we must hold everything loosely, because when I grip it tightly, it hurts when the Father pries my fingers loose and takes it from me!"[5]

Another experienced disciple, A. W. Tozer, gave this seasoned advice on possessions.

> There can be no doubt that this possessive cling-ing to things is one of the most harmful habits in the life. Because it is so natural, it is rarely recognized for the evil that it is. But its outworkings are tragic.
>
> We are often hindered from giving up our trea-sures to the Lord out of fear for their safety. This is especially true when those treasures are loved rela-tives and friends. But we need have no such fears. Our Lord came not to destroy but to save. Every-thing is safe which we commit to Him, and nothing is really safe which is not so committed. . . .
>
> . . . The ancient curse will not go out painlessly; the tough, old miser within us will not lie down and die in obedience to our command. He must be torn out of our heart like a plant from the soil; he must be extracted in agony and blood like a tooth from the jaw. He must be expelled from our soul by vio-lence, as Christ expelled the money changers from

---

5. As told to Charles R. Swindoll and quoted by him in *Living Above the Level of Mediocrity* (Waco, Tex.: Word Books, 1987), p. 114.

the temple. And we shall need to steel ourselves against his piteous begging, and to recognize it as springing out of self-pity, one of the most reprehensible sins of the human heart.[6]

The Reasons for Consecration

To many people then and today, Jesus' requirements for discipleship may seem too strict and unyielding. And our natural response is to ask *why*. Why does discipleship have to be so exacting? Jesus used two stories to explain why such terms are necessary.

> "For which one of you, when he wants to build a tower, does not first sit down and calculate the cost, to see if he has enough to complete it? Otherwise, when he has laid a foundation, and is not able to finish, all who observe it begin to ridicule him, saying, 'This man began to build and was not able to finish.' Or what king, when he sets out to meet another king in battle, will not first sit down and take counsel whether he is strong enough with ten thousand men to encounter the one coming against him with twenty thousand? Or else, while the other is still far away, he sends a delegation and asks terms of peace." (vv. 28–32)

In *Living Above the Level of Mediocrity*, the meaning of this passage is examined.

> These two stories explain why Christ spoke in such stringent terms to the crowd. The first has to do with *building* and the second, with *fighting*. In each case, Jesus emphasizes the importance of quality. In building a tower that will last, quality builders are essential. And they cost a lot. In fighting a battle, quality soldiers (not the quantity of them, please notice) are all-important. They, too, are costly.
>
> For years I taught that *we* are to "count the cost." It seemed so plausible. But suddenly one day, it

6. A. W. Tozer, *The Pursuit of God*, Tozer Legacy ed. (Camp Hill, Pa.: Christian Publications, 1982), pp. 28–30.

dawned on me that Jesus never once told His followers to count the cost. No—*He's* the One who has already done that. He is the "king" (v. 31) who has already determined what it will take to encounter and triumph over life's enemies. And what *will* it take? A few strong, quality-minded champions whose commitment is solid as stone. And the cost will be great.[7]

The Summary

In closing, Jesus preserves His teaching and its importance in the minds of the people with the illustration of a natural preservative—salt.

> "Therefore, salt is good; but if even salt has become tasteless, with what will it be seasoned? It is useless either for the soil or for the manure pile; it is thrown out. He who has ears to hear, let him hear." (vv. 34–35)

Jesus' listeners knew that one of the primary uses of salt was to preserve, to retard corruption. And they also knew that when salt

> loses its essential quality and fails to perform its essential duty, it is fit for nothing but to be thrown away.[8]

Likewise, Jesus warned, to cease obeying His terms for discipleship would mean we would lose our essential Christlike qualities and fail to perform the essential duties we were created for (see Eph. 2:10).

For those of you willing to accept Jesus' terms of discipleship, perhaps the most appropriate way to close our study and begin following Him is through prayer.

> O God, I have tasted Thy goodness, and it has both satisfied me and made me thirsty for more. I am painfully conscious of my need of further grace. I am ashamed of my lack of desire. O God, the

---

7. Swindoll, *Mediocrity*, p. 56.

8. William Barclay, *The Gospel of Luke*, rev. ed., The Daily Study Bible Series (Philadelphia, Pa.: Westminster Press, 1975), p. 197.

Triune God, I want to want Thee; I long to be filled with longing; I thirst to be made more thirsty still. Show me Thy glory, I pray Thee, that so I may know Thee indeed. Begin in mercy a new work of love within me. Say to my soul, "Rise up, my love, my fair one, and come away." Then give me grace to rise and follow Thee up from this misty lowland where I have wandered so long. In Jesus' name. Amen.[9]

 ## *Living Insights*

Robert Frost wrote,

> Two roads diverged in a wood, and I—
> I took the one less traveled by,
> And that has made all the difference.[10]

Being confronted with the cost of discipleship is like coming to Frost's fork in the road. Only now we must choose between the road less traveled—discipleship on Jesus' terms—and the road that meanders according to our own terms.

When you look back a week from now, a year, which road will you be on? Fill in your own version of "The Road Not Taken":

> I shall be telling this with a sigh
> Somewhere ages and ages hence:
> Two roads diverged in a wood, and I—
> I took _____,
> And that has made all the difference.

 ## *Living Insights*

In his book *Who Switched the Price Tags?* Tony Campolo recalls the time he and a childhood buddy came up with "a brilliant and creative plan for mischief."

---

9. Tozer, *The Pursuit of God*, p. 20.

10. Robert Frost, "The Road Not Taken," in *Robert Frost's Poems*, introduction and commentary by Louis Untermeyer (New York, N.Y.: Washington Square Press, Pocket Books, 1971), p. 223.

Our plan was to get into that five-and-dime store and *change the price tags* on things.

We imagined what it would be like the next morning when people came into the store and discovered that radios were selling for a quarter and bobby pins were priced at five dollars each. With diabolical glee, we wondered what it would be like in that store when nobody could figure out what the prices of things really should be.

Sometimes I think that Satan has played the same kind of trick on all of us. Sometimes I think that he has broken into our lives and changed the price tags on things. Too often, under the influences of his malicious ploy, we treat what deserves to be treated with loving care as though it were of little worth. On the other hand, we find ourselves tempted to make great sacrifices for that which, in the long run of life, has no lasting value. . . . Sometimes I think that one of the worst consequences of being fallen creatures is our failure to understand what really is important in life.[11]

Sometimes we do put a higher price tag on relationships, self, and possessions than we do on following Christ. Let's take some time now to check our price tags in each of the three terms for discipleship. You may discover some that need changing.

- Under each term of discipleship, write a summary of it and then answer the question following.

Personal Relationships

Summary: _____

_____

_____

_____

11. Anthony Campolo, *Who Switched the Price Tags?* (Waco, Tex.: Word Books, 1986), pp. 13, 14.

Is there someone whose friendship pressures me to back off from my obedience to Christ? If so, who and why?

_____

_____

_____

Personal Goals and Desires

Summary: _____

_____

_____

_____

Is there a personal desire I have not been willing to put to death to follow Christ? If so, what?

_____

_____

_____

Personal Possessions

Summary: _____

_____

_____

_____

Is there anything that I put greater value on than Christ?

_____

_____

_____

Chapter 6

STIMULUS OF DISCIPLESHIP... IMPARTATION

John 13:33–14:6, Mark 6:31–52, Luke 11:1–4

For three years, wherever Jesus went, His gaggle of disciples followed. But it wasn't simply following Him that caused the Lord's faithlings to grow. Rather, they were stimulated to grow because Jesus constantly combined their being together with the practice of impartation—the ability to pluck spiritual truths from daily occurrences to feed the disciples.

By giving sight to a man blind from birth, Jesus gave the disciples the truth "I am the light of the world" to chew on. While more than five thousand people ate their fill from two fish and five loaves, the disciples supped on the truth that with Jesus nothing was impossible. And they nearly choked on the abundance of food for thought when Jesus declared He was the resurrection and the life and then raised up Lazarus, who had been dead for four days. A day didn't go by that the disciples weren't stimulated to grow through something Jesus imparted by word or deed.

But *that* was Jesus. Many of you may wonder, What can *I* impart to my disciples today? A key for unlocking some answers to that question is found in John 14.

On the night before His crucifixion, Jesus told the disciples He was going to leave and they could not follow Him (John 13:33). He told the disciples that one of them was going to betray Him and that another, Peter, a leader within that small circle of followers, would deny Him not once but three times (vv. 21, 36–38). Knowing that these were hard words to digest for disciples still so young in their faith, Jesus sought to comfort them.

> "Let not your heart be troubled; believe in God, believe also in Me. In My Father's house are many dwelling places; if it were not so, I would have told you; for I go to prepare a place for you. And if I go and prepare a place for you, I will come again, and receive you to Myself; that where I am, there you

may be also. And you know the way where I am going." (14:1–4)

"Way? What way?" Thomas wondered (see v. 5). And he knew by the look on the rest of the disciples' faces that they didn't know the way Jesus was going either. So Jesus gave His disciples, and all the world, specific directions to His Father's house.

Jesus said to him, "I am the way, and the truth, and the life; no one comes to the Father, but through Me." (v. 6)

Though not normally associated with discipleship, Jesus' three crucial words—*way, truth,* and *life*—provide a helpful outline for understanding the whole subject of impartation. We want to glean from these words not the way of salvation, but rather directions to disciples for drawing near to God.

General Definitions

Bible scholar Merrill Tenney said,

Christianity is not a system of philosophy, nor a ritual, nor a code of laws; it is the impartation of a divine vitality. Without the way there is no going, without the truth there is no knowing, without the life there is no living.[1]

Let's take a moment to briefly define, from a discipleship perspective, three characteristics of impartation—the way, the truth, and the life.

The Way. Basic to the survival of all disciples is the ability to find God's way for their lives. As disciplers, we must impart to those we're discipling the techniques involved in discovering and entering into the will of God.[2]

The Truth. Every discipler is primarily a teacher—someone who provides truths, insights, and practical techniques for learning and applying God's Word.[3]

1. Merrill C. Tenney, *John: The Gospel of Belief* (Grand Rapids, Mich.: William B. Eerdmans Publishing Co., 1948), pp. 215–16.

2. For further study on the will of God, read Garry Friesen's excellent book *Decision Making and the Will of God.*

3. For help in learning how to teach effectively, read Howard Hendricks' book *Teaching to Change Lives.*

The Life. The third aspect of impartation is what makes it so effective. The ones doing the discipling demonstrate Christ and His truths with their own lives! The disciple is given an indelible set of human and divine notes from a living text.[4]

Specific Observations

Now let's dig deeper to see how Jesus imparted the way, the truth, and the life to His disciples.

The Way: Direction

Impartation involves giving disciples direction on how to discover God's will for their lives. Here are three facets of communicating this direction.

Imparting direction involves helping disciples reach their full potential. Jesus sees men and women not only as they are, but also as they are to become. And in conveying that insight, disciples are given tremendous direction in understanding God's will for their lives. Simon Peter probably thought his potential stretched only as far as he could throw a fishing net. But Jesus saw something different.

> One of the two who . . . followed Him, was Andrew, Simon Peter's brother. He found first his own brother Simon, and said to him, "We have found the Messiah" (which translated means Christ). He brought him to Jesus. Jesus looked at him, and said, "You are Simon the son of John; you shall be called Cephas" (which translated means Peter). (1:40–42)

Beneath this fisherman's sunburned exterior, Jesus could see rocklike potential, so He renamed him Peter, meaning *rock.* However, *we* aren't like Jesus—we can't size up a person's potential at a glance. That's the value of discipleship. It provides us with close interpersonal relationships where we can help others see and develop their full potential.

Imparting direction involves helping people set goals for their lives. Jesus not only called Peter and Andrew to be His disciples, He immediately set before them a clear goal for living.

> And Jesus said to them, "Follow Me, and I will make you become fishers of men." (Mark 1:17)

---

4. For further study in this area, read *Life-Style Evangelism* by Joseph Aldrich.

46

Did you notice how Jesus put the goal into terms they could easily relate to—"fishers of men"? The duty of every discipler is to help the disciple articulate and act upon clear goals for life, family, the study of the Word, and other important areas.

Imparting direction involves helping a disciple maintain a balance between activity and rest. When Jesus' disciples rehuddled after their first attempts as missionaries, Jesus saw that they were tired, so He called for a time-out.

> And He said to them, "Come away by yourselves to a lonely place and rest a while." (For there were many people coming and going, and they did not even have time to eat.) And they went away in the boat to a lonely place by themselves. (6:31–32)

Whether it's a time for relaxing our souls, our bodies, or both, every disciple needs to be taught how to balance rest and activity. Elton Trueblood said,

> The man who supposes that he has no time to pray or to reflect, because the social tasks are numerous and urgent, will soon find that he has become fundamentally unproductive, because he will have separated his life from its roots.[5]

The Truth: Declaration

In our schools today we're conditioned to learn by bells. Bells tell us when to begin and when to stop thinking about a particular subject and move on to the next. In a discipling relationship, however, truth is not imparted between bells. Jesus never rang a bell to signal He was about to teach something. For the disciples, class was always in session.

Let's pick up where we left off in Mark 6 with Jesus moving His twelve tired pupils to a secluded spot for some rest. What follows is a perfect example of how Jesus seized opportunities for imparting truth. The disciples thought they were going to receive rest; what they got was a lesson on faith.

> And the people saw them going, and many recognized them, and they ran there together on foot from all

---

5. Elton Trueblood, *The New Man for Our Time* (New York, N.Y.: Harper and Row, Publishers, 1970), p. 60.

47

the cities, and got there ahead of them. And when He went ashore, He saw a great multitude, and He felt compassion for them because they were like sheep without a shepherd; and He began to teach them many things. And when it was already quite late, His disciples came up to Him and began saying, "The place is desolate and it is already quite late; send them away so that they may go into the surrounding countryside and villages and buy themselves something to eat." (vv. 33–36)

Since the disciples were tired even before the crowds showed up, you can imagine that by this time they were getting a little irritable. "Tell them to go *home*, Lord!" But beyond the growling stomachs, tired faces, and late hour, Jesus saw the right setting for imparting an important truth: "Is anything too difficult for the Lord?" (Gen. 18:14a; see also Mark 10:27b).

But He answered and said to them, "You give them something to eat!" And they said to Him, "Shall we go and spend two hundred denarii on bread and give them something to eat?" And He said to them, "How many loaves do you have? Go look!" And when they found out, they said, "Five and two fish." And He commanded them all to recline by groups on the green grass. And they reclined in companies of hundreds and of fifties. And He took the five loaves and the two fish, and looking up toward heaven, He blessed the food and broke the loaves and He kept giving them to the disciples to set before them; and He divided up the two fish among them all. And they all ate and were satisfied. And they picked up twelve full baskets of the broken pieces, and also of the fish. (Mark 6:37–43)

What a lesson! More than five thousand people miraculously fed with enough leftovers to fill twelve baskets—a physical object lesson on trusting in Him. The disciples *really* understood faith after that, right? Let's find out.

And immediately He made His disciples get into the boat and go ahead of Him to the other side to Bethsaida, while He Himself was sending the multitude away. And after bidding them farewell, He departed to the mountain to pray. And when it was evening, the boat was in the midst of the sea, and He was alone on the land. And seeing them straining at the oars, for the wind was against them, at about the fourth watch of the night, He came to them, walking on the sea; and He intended to pass by them. But when they saw Him walking on the sea, they supposed that it was a ghost, and cried out; for they all saw Him and were frightened. But immediately He spoke with them and said to them, "Take courage; it is I, do not be afraid." And He got into the boat with them, and the wind stopped; and they were greatly astonished. (vv. 45–51)

Why were the disciples astonished? Hadn't they just seen Jesus feed all those people? Yes, but somewhere in the passing out of all that food the disciples' minds strayed and missed Jesus' point. It would take many more practical lessons on faith, just like this impromptu one on the lake, for the disciples to learn.

For they had not gained any insight from the incident of the loaves, but their heart was hardened. (v. 52)

From this we discover an essential facet of imparting truth: patience!

The Life: Demonstration

A third powerful way of imparting something is with our lives, how we live. In Luke 11, Jesus didn't announce to His disciples, "Today, the subject is prayer." He simply prayed. And like little children, the disciples watched Him and then wanted to learn how to pray as He did.

And it came about that while He was praying in a certain place, after He had finished, one of His disciples said to Him, "Lord, teach us to pray just as John also taught his disciples." And He said to them, "When you pray, say:

'Father, hallowed be Thy name.
Thy kingdom come.
Give us each day our daily bread.

And forgive us our sins,
For we ourselves also forgive everyone who
    is indebted to us.
And lead us not into temptation.' "
(vv. 1–4)

In his book *Teaching to Change Lives,* Howard Hendricks considers an ancient Chinese proverb:

I hear, and I forget.
I see, and I remember.
I do, and I understand.

I would make one addition to that proverb. In
my judgment, when you *do,* the result is more than
understanding; you also *change.*[6]

Jesus didn't simply give the disciples five helpful tips on prayer, He helped them connect prayer with life by modeling it for them. It was His life that prompted the disciples' desire to learn how to pray.

Prompting others to learn from following a personal example wasn't something only Jesus could do. The apostle Paul, for example, wrote:

The things you have learned and received and heard
and seen in me, practice these things; and the God
of peace shall be with you. (Phil. 4:9)

Whether we're teaching in a discipleship setting or from a podium or a lectern, our lives as well as our words are constantly being studied. This is why James says that teachers will be judged by a stricter standard—our lives *are* our teaching (see James 3:1)!

Summary

Thomas said, "Lord, we don't know the way." Today there are many Thomases sitting in pews who need someone to show them the way. The greatest legacy of any Christian is not to be remembered simply as a great speaker or theologian. The richest legacy for any of us to leave behind is trained disciples who are reared on the three methods of impartation: direction, declaration, and demonstration. What will your legacy be?

6. Howard G. Hendricks, *Teaching to Change Lives* (Portland, Oreg.: Multnomah Press, 1987), p. 81.

From a chapter titled "The Law of Activity," Howard Hendricks says,

> Psychologists tell us we have the potential of remembering only up to 10 percent of what we hear. And that's *potential,* not actual. As a matter of fact, if you do remember 10 percent of what you hear you're in the genius category.
>
> Unfortunately, the bulk of Christian education is hearing-oriented. . . .
>
> If we add seeing to hearing, psychologists say our potential for remembering goes up to 50 percent.[7]

Ever wonder what kind of impact Jesus' life would have had on the disciples had He only taught them inside a temple for three years? Never any healings, only descriptions of them. Never any real moments of compassion—the woman caught in adultery, the father with a demon-possessed son—only imaginary moments fixed on scrolls of papyrus. Never any excited crowds, sermons on mountainsides, or miracles at tombs. Just the disciples sitting in the same temple seats day after day, listening.

Fortunately, the disciples *saw* Jesus pray. They witnessed Him reaching out to the leper, feeding the hungry, and driving the money changers from the temple. One life rubbing off on others—demonstration. Then Jesus sent them out to minister as they had seen Him do (see Mark 6:7–13). Hendricks adds,

> What about adding *doing* to seeing and hearing? The psychologists say this combination brings the percentage of memory up to 90 percent—and decades of teaching in a graduate institution have given me all the evidence I need to be convinced that's exactly true.[8]

Is your discipleship ministry too hearing-oriented? How much of Christ are you imparting that your disciple, children, or spouse will remember? Eight percent or eighty?

7. Hendricks, *Teaching to Change Lives,* p. 81.

8. Hendricks, *Teaching to Change Lives,* p. 82.

Take some time now to brainstorm as many specific ways of demonstrating Christ and the spiritual disciplines as you can.

_____

_____

_____

_____

_____

_____

_____

_____

You're up to 50 percent, now let's go for 90. Go back over your list and write down practical ways of enabling your disciples to do what they have seen you do.

_____

_____

_____

_____

_____

_____

_____

_____

 ## *Living Insights* STUDY TWO

Let's turn the first Living Insight around. What if Jesus had never communicated any truth to His disciples? What if they had seen and done everything just as it's recorded in the Scriptures, but without any teaching? The New Testament would be nothing more than a travelogue about a very unusual man. The true meaning of Jesus' life and death would be totally lost, and mankind right along with it.

Demonstration divorced from truth is out of balance. Without biblical truth we would lose both our identity as His disciples and our way (see John 8:31–32 and Ps. 119:105). Romans 10:17 says,

> So faith comes from hearing, and hearing by the word of Christ.

- Take a moment to examine the balance between truth and demonstration in your discipling. Are you imparting the "word of Christ"?

How often? _____

_____

What aspect of the word of Christ? _____

_____

In case you need help in this area, here are just a few suggestions to get you started.

Visit with your pastor or others who know the Scriptures well and ask for their recommendations. You might also check at the local Christian bookstore for Bible study materials. In particular, the Navigators have excellent discipleship study helps available.

Chapter 7

BADGE OF DISCIPLESHIP...
AFFECTION

John 13:1–35

In *The Mark of a Christian,* Francis Schaeffer wrote,

> Through the centuries men have displayed many different symbols to show that they are Christians. They have worn marks in the lapels of their coats, hung chains about their necks, even had special haircuts.
>
> Of course, there is nothing wrong with any of this. . . . But there is a much better sign—a mark that has not been thought up just as a matter of expediency for use on some special occasion or in some specific era. It is a universal mark that is to last through all the ages of the church till Jesus comes back.[1]

Chuck Colson reveals what this mark is with a candid personal story that took place inside a state penitentiary's death row.

> My schedule was extremely tight, so after we finished "Amazing Grace" we said our good-byes and began filing out. We were crowded into the caged area between the two massive gates when we noticed one volunteer had stayed back and was with James Brewer in his cell. I went to get the man because the warden could not operate the gates until we had all cleared out.
>
> "I'm sorry, we have to leave," I said, looking nervously at my watch, knowing a plane stood waiting at a nearby airstrip to fly me to Indianapolis to meet with Governor Orr. The volunteer, a short

---

1. Francis A. Schaeffer, *The Mark of the Christian* (Downers Grove, Ill.: InterVarsity Press, 1970), p. 7.

white man in his early fifties, was standing shoulder to shoulder with Brewer. The prisoner was holding his Bible open while the older man appeared to be reading a verse.

"Oh, yes," the volunteer looked up. "Give us just a minute, please. This is important," he added softly.

"No, I'm sorry," I snapped. "I can't keep the governor waiting. We must go."

"I understand," the man said, still speaking softly, "but this is important. You see, I'm Judge Clement. I'm the man who sentenced James here to die. But now he's my brother and we want a minute to pray together."

I stood frozen in the cell doorway. It didn't matter who I kept waiting. . . . Anywhere other than the kingdom of God, that inmate might have killed that judge with his bare hands—or wanted to anyway. Now they were one, their faces reflecting an indescribable expression of love as they prayed together.[2]

Colson calls this *frontline love*. It's the kind of affection Jesus showed His disciples. And it's the badge of discipleship that He wants all His followers to wear.

To put on this badge, we must first learn to love as Jesus taught His disciples to love during their last supper together. And none of the gospel writers relates that night with such sensitive detail as John. Let's go back to that second-story room in Jerusalem and see through John's eyes how Jesus stitched into the disciples' hearts—between the eating, arguing, and the questioning—the badge of discipleship, affection.

The Setting

Before opening the door to the intimate scene of his last meal with the Savior, John acquaints us with what was happening in Jerusalem, in the Savior's heart, and in the heart of a betrayer.

> Now before the Feast of the Passover, Jesus knowing that His hour had come that He should depart

2. Charles W. Colson, *Loving God* (Grand Rapids, Mich.: Zondervan Publishing House, Judith Markham Books, 1983), pp. 193–94.

out of this world to the Father, having loved His own who were in the world, He loved them to the end. And during supper, the devil having already put into the heart of Judas Iscariot, the son of Simon, to betray Him, Jesus, knowing that the Father had given all things into His hands, and that He had come forth from God, and was going back to God . . . (John 13:1–3)

With his own sensitive eye for detail, Ken Gire takes us behind the scenes of these first three verses.

As the disciples prepare for Passover, Jerusalem is brimming with religious pilgrims who have poured into the holy city to celebrate the feast. It is a sacred time for the Jew. A time to look back—back to the nation's deliverance from the tight-knuckled, four-hundred-year grip of Egyptian bondage. It is also a time to look forward—forward to the time when the Messiah will come to usher in an unprecedented era of blessing.

This Passover, Jesus and the Twelve withdraw to an upper room. It is a quiet respite from tonight's teeming crowds—and from the turbulent storm that awaits tomorrow.

In his soul Jesus feels the sharp winds which harbinger that storm. He feels the chill of betrayal, of desertion, of denial.

Jesus and the disciples gather around a low table to celebrate the feast. John reclines to the right of Jesus; Judas, to the left at the place of honor. They stretch slantwise on padded mats, propping themselves on the left arm, leaving the other free to handle the food.

Each portion they handle is a sermoned echo of the nation's first Passover. The bowl of bitter herbs, vinegar, and salt is a reminder of the bitter years of slavery. The flat cakes of yeastless bread are a reminder of their hurried exodus. And finally, there is the roasted lamb, a symbol of deliverance. . . .

Tonight, Jesus is celebrating the feast an evening early. For tomorrow, when the nation will be preparing its Passover lambs, God will be preparing his. An innocent lamb, without spot or blemish . . . led to the slaughter, silent before its shearers . . . stricken, pierced for our transgressions.[3]

Crowded together in John's memory of that last meal are feelings of excitement, anger, shame, and more. But above all, he remembers how Christ loved the disciples "to the end" (v. 1). He remembers how the Lamb of God wasn't so preoccupied with His imminent death that He forgot to share the kind of affection He wanted the disciples to emulate. An affection that reached toward insiders, potential insiders, and outsiders.

Demonstration of Affection

Because there were no sidewalks or paved streets in the first century, it was customary for people to have their feet washed as they entered someone's home. Typically, a servant would meet the guests at the door, remove their sandals, and wash and dry their feet. And if there was no servant, a volunteer would perform the task.

Yet when the disciples reclined to share the Passover meal with Jesus, none of their feet had been washed. They were without a servant, and no one volunteered for the foot-washing job. Why? Dr. Luke helps us here, for he included in his gospel narrative of this meal a significant detail that John leaves out. According to Luke 22:24, the disciples were too puffed up with pride, arguing about which of them was the greatest, to consider washing feet.

Toward the Insider . . . Humility

The pride drained from the disciples' voices. The arguing stopped. And they watched in shame as Jesus assumed the role they would not.

> [Jesus] rose from supper, and laid aside His garments; and taking a towel, He girded Himself about. Then He poured water into the basin, and began to wash the disciples' feet, and to wipe them with the towel with which He was girded. (John 13:4–5)

---

3. Ken Gire, *Intimate Moments with the Savior* (Grand Rapids, Mich.: Zondervan Publishing House, Daybreak Books, 1989), pp. 88–90.

Who was the greatest? No one cared anymore as they each had their feet washed by the Master. Then Jesus explained the principle of showing affection through humility.

> And so when He had washed their feet, and taken His garments, and reclined at the table again, He said to them, "Do you know what I have done to you? You call Me Teacher and Lord; and you are right, for so I am. If I then, the Lord and the Teacher, washed your feet, you also ought to wash one another's feet. For I gave you an example that you also should do as I did to you. Truly, truly, I say to you, a slave is not greater than his master; neither is one who is sent greater than the one who sent him. If you know these things, you are blessed if you do them." (vv. 12–17)

The badge of discipleship becomes visible each time we relate to our inner circle of Christian friends with humility (see Gal. 5:13, Phil. 2:1–5). It is through stooping, seeking to serve others before ourselves, that Jesus' promise for genuine happiness is fulfilled. Pride, on the other hand, will always seek to convince us that stooping is a ridiculous posture and that serving ourselves should be our first priority. We must decide whom we will follow: our pride or Jesus.

Toward the Potential Insider . . . Acceptance

Jesus also directed His affection toward potential insiders, people who would become members of that inner family of believers in the future.

> "Truly, truly, I say to you, he who receives whomever I send receives Me; and he who receives Me receives Him who sent Me." (John 13:20)

Jesus told His disciples to be sure to receive, to welcome, those who would believe in Him after He was gone. Christ wants His church to be a place of acceptance, not exclusivism.

Jesus knew His disciples needed to be encouraged to show their affection in this way, because they had failed at it before. Several months earlier they had mistakenly tried to exclude someone from ministering simply because he was not a part of the Twelve (see Luke 9:49–50). But rather than hoarding our faith and affection,

Jesus wants His disciples to be known for the way in which they freely give both away.

Toward the Outsider . . . Tolerance

The final direction in which Jesus' affection flows is toward an outsider—Judas.

> When Jesus had said this, He became troubled in spirit, and testified, and said, "Truly, truly, I say to you, that one of you will betray Me." The disciples began looking at one another, at a loss to know of which one He was speaking. There was reclining on Jesus' breast one of His disciples, whom Jesus loved. Simon Peter therefore gestured to him, and said to him, "Tell us who it is of whom He is speaking." He, leaning back thus on Jesus' breast, said to Him, "Lord, who is it?" Jesus therefore answered, "That is the one for whom I shall dip the morsel and give it to him." So when He had dipped the morsel, He took and gave it to Judas, the son of Simon Iscariot. (John 13:21–26; see also vv. 27–30)

Again, let's follow along with Ken Gire as he transports us into this tense moment in the Upper Room.

> It was customary for the master of the feast to put bits of lamb onto a piece of unleavened bread, dip it into the bitter herb sauce, and hand it to his guests. And it was customary to offer the first piece to the most honored guest.
>
> He hands the bread to Judas . . . to take . . . and to eat.
>
> The dramatic moment is not only an unmasking of the traitor but a final offer of salvation. Judas's pulse quickens and his face flushes hot and red. For an awkward moment, the eyes of the betrayer and the betrayed meet. A knife of regret cuts an opening in Judas's soul. Haltingly, he takes the rolled-up piece of bread. But he can't quite bring it to his mouth. Sweat gathers at his hairline. He bites his lip.
>
> From the shadows Satan sees the quivering hand. He sees his pawn is vulnerable. The Prince of Darkness counters with a strategic move and enters Judas.

The disciple puts down the bread and reaches for his pouch. The opening is closed. The pawn is safe.

"What you are about to do, do quickly."

With those words, Jesus seals his fate. And the fate of Judas. They would both go their separate ways. To separate trees. To separate destinies.[4]

Jesus handed the morsel to Judas. It was a gracious act of tolerance, a way of saying to Judas that He was still willing to allow him to change if he wanted to. In this single act, Christ bequeathed to His disciples the responsibility to temper their response toward unbelievers with tolerance, not prejudice. Prejudice causes believers to withhold affection. When we assume that a lost person will not respond to our affection, we fail to offer any. But Jesus' offer of affection wasn't based on how Judas was going to respond. It sprang from Christ's unconditional love for the lost, which should be our source as well.

Instruction on Affection

Finally, Jesus rolls up the affection that the disciples have seen and heard since the beginning of the meal and hands it to them in a command.

> "A new commandment I give to you, that you love one another, even as I have loved you, that you also love one another. By this all men will know that you are My disciples, if you have love for one another." (vv. 34–35)

Jesus wants His disciples, then and now, to do more than simply remember the affection He shared that night. He wants us to *practice* this kind of affection, to wear the badge of discipleship through humility, acceptance, and tolerance.

 Living Insights ⎯⎯⎯⎯⎯⎯⎯⎯⎯⎯ STUDY ONE

For those of you wanting to study the badge of discipleship more deeply with your disciple, try this:

---

4. Gire, *Intimate Moments with the Savior,* pp. 91–92.

60

- First, compare the foot washing in John 13:4–17 with Luke 7:36–50.

Contrasts

John 13:4–17   Luke 7:36–50

_____   _____
_____   _____
_____   _____
_____   _____

Similarities

_____
_____
_____
_____

- Next, notice in the Luke passage who exemplified each of the expressions of love covered in this study and who exemplified their opposites.

Expressions of Love   **Opposites of Love**

Humility _____   Pride _____

Acceptance _____   Rejection _____

Tolerance _____   Prejudice _____

You might also want to focus on personal applications, asking each other questions such as, Which mark of affection characterizes my love for others most? Least?

- Finally, what are some practical ways you and the person you're discipling can encourage each other to be humble and show acceptance and tolerance?

_____
_____
_____
_____

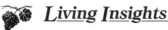 **_Living Insights_**

For many Christians, wearing the badge of affection is most difficult in the battle trenches of disagreements—especially when fellow believers are dug in on either side. Francis Schaeffer wrote,

> I have observed one thing *among true Christians* in their differences in many countries: What divides and severs true Christian groups and Christians— what leaves a bitterness that can last for 20, 30 or 40 years . . . is not the issue of doctrine or belief which caused the differences in the first place. Invariably it is lack of love—and the bitter things that are said by true Christians in the midst of differences. These stick in the mind like glue. . . . It is these things—these unloving attitudes and words— that cause the stench that the world can smell in the church of Jesus Christ among those who are really true Christians.[5]

How do we rid ourselves of this stench and replace it with the fragrance of Christ's love? One way to begin is by remembering to do something that all of us are familiar with but few practice.

> When I have made a mistake and when I have failed to love my Christian brother, I go to him and say, "I'm sorry." That is first.
>   It may seem a letdown—that the first thing we speak of should be so simple! But if you think it is easy, you have never tried to practice it.[6]

- Do you need to tell someone you're sorry? Your spouse? Your child? A work colleague? A neighbor? Who?

_____

_____

_____

_____

5. Schaeffer, *The Mark of the Christian*, pp. 22–23.
6. Schaeffer, *The Mark of the Christian*, p. 21.

Admitting when you're wrong will nurture humility, foster acceptance, and encourage tolerance. And above all, it will replace the stench of pride with the fragrance of Christ's affection. Paul said,

> Therefore be imitators of God, as beloved children; and walk in love, just as Christ also loved you, and gave Himself up for us, an offering and a sacrifice to God as a fragrant aroma. (Eph. 5:1–2)

Chapter 8

GENIUS OF DISCIPLESHIP...
DELEGATION

Exodus 18:13–27; Matthew 9:35–10:19, 17:14–20

Samuel Langhorne Clemens had a knack for telling familiar maxims in a fresh and humorous way. For example, see if you can recognize the old saying behind our lesson today in this personal quip.

> When I was a boy of fourteen, my father was so ignorant I could hardly stand to have the old man around. But when I got to be twenty-one, I was astonished at how much the old man had learned in seven years.[1]

The adage that Mr. Clemens, better known as Mark Twain, is tickling your ribs about is: "Experience is the best teacher." It's a good statement, but not altogether accurate. Besides having costly fees, the school of experience relies on the quirky teaching method of testing you first and then teaching the lesson. A better teacher is *guided* experience—delegation. Delegation involves guiding another's growth by combining helpful information and techniques with assigned responsibilities. In a discipleship framework, delegation enables disciples to mature through successfully combining their knowledge with actual practice.

Delegation Illustrated

In today's study we'll learn lessons from Moses first, then Jesus, which will show how the guided experience that delegation offers is the best teacher.

Moses

Moses was a strong leader but a weak discipler. Like many great leaders, he was faithful to the task, a hard worker, and genuinely capable. So capable, in fact, that he was blinded to the importance of allowing others to shoulder Israel's leadership needs.

1. *The International Dictionary of Thoughts,* comp. John P. Bradley, Leo F. Daniels, Thomas C. Jones (Chicago, Ill.: J. G. Ferguson Publishing Co., 1969), p. 270.

Another great leader, Dwight L. Moody, once said that he "would rather put a thousand men to work than do the work of a thousand men."[2] Moses, however, attempted to do the work of a thousand men while a thousand men with leadership potential stood by watching.

The individual who opened Moses' eyes to the need for delegating was Jethro, his father-in-law. Jethro had come to visit Moses, and like a proud father-in-law, he went with Moses to watch him work. What Jethro saw was that Moses had a good heart, but he needed some fatherly advice about delegating.

> And it came about the next day that Moses sat to judge the people, and the people stood about Moses from the morning until the evening. Now when Moses' father-in-law saw all that he was doing for the people, he said, "What is this thing that you are doing for the people? Why do you alone sit as judge and all the people stand about you from morning until evening?" And Moses said to his father-in-law, "Because the people come to me to inquire of God. When they have a dispute, it comes to me, and I judge between a man and his neighbor, and make known the statutes of God and His laws." And Moses' father-in-law said to him, "The thing that you are doing is not good. You will surely wear out, both yourself and these people who are with you, for the task is too heavy for you; you cannot do it alone." (Exod. 18:13–18)

First Jethro presented Moses with the down side of his Lone Ranger leadership style. "Moses, you're going to exhaust yourself and exasperate the people." Then this sympathetic and wise man offered Moses some shrewd counsel on how to share the leadership reins with others.

> "Now listen to me: I shall give you counsel, and God be with you. You be the people's representative before God, and you bring the disputes to God, then teach them the statutes and the laws, and make

2. As quoted by J. Oswald Sanders in *Spiritual Leadership*, rev. ed. (Chicago, Ill.: Moody Press, 1980), p. 167.

known to them the way in which they are to walk, and the work they are to do. Furthermore, you shall select out of all the people able men who fear God, men of truth, those who hate dishonest gain; and you shall place these over them, as leaders of thousands, of hundreds, of fifties and of tens. And let them judge the people at all times; and let it be that every major dispute they will bring to you, but every minor dispute they themselves will judge. So it will be easier for you, and they will bear the burden with you. If you do this thing and God so commands you, then you will be able to endure, and all these people also will go to their place in peace." (vv. 19–23)

It's easy to understand why Moses was used to leading Israel alone. He alone had been chosen to speak for God, to confront Pharaoh, and to lead the people out of Egypt. And it would have been a great temptation for anyone in his position to refuse to share that leadership with others. But Moses wasn't interested in playing "king of the hill." He was God's servant before he was Israel's leader.

So Moses listened to his father-in-law, and did all that he had said. And Moses chose able men out of all Israel, and made them heads over the people, leaders of thousands, of hundreds, of fifties and of tens. And they judged the people at all times; the difficult dispute they would bring to Moses, but every minor dispute they themselves would judge. Then Moses bade his father-in-law farewell, and he went his way into his own land. (vv. 24–27)

Jesus

Now let's turn our attention to the individual whose method of discipleship was the paradigm of delegation—Jesus Christ.

And Jesus was going about all the cities and the villages, teaching in their synagogues, and proclaiming the gospel of the kingdom, and healing every kind of disease and every kind of sickness. (Matt. 9:35)

The disciples have been with Jesus for some time now. And so far their only involvement has been to listen and observe. But that is about to change.

> And seeing the multitudes, He felt compassion for them, because they were distressed and downcast like sheep without a shepherd. Then He said to His disciples, "The harvest is plentiful, but the workers are few. Therefore beseech the Lord of the harvest to send out workers into His harvest." (vv. 36–38)

Here is the beginning of Christ's ministry of delegation. First, He asks His disciples to get involved by sharing His burden to pray for workers. And when that's been done, He calls them to action.

> And having summoned His twelve disciples, He gave them authority over unclean spirits, to cast them out, and to heal every kind of disease and every kind of sickness. . . .
>
> These twelve Jesus sent out after instructing them, saying, "Do not go in the way of the Gentiles, and do not enter any city of the Samaritans; but rather go to the lost sheep of the house of Israel. And as you go, preach, saying, 'The kingdom of heaven is at hand.'" (10:1, 5–7)

Jesus' fledgling disciples were growing up. It was time for them to leave the nest and, under Christ's careful guidance, test their wings for ministering on their own. It was a whole new phase of training, one that would continue their transformation into apostles —disciples capable of carrying on the ministry and training others.[3]

Also, note the pattern in the ministry of delegation. Christ didn't call His disciples and immediately put them out on the front lines of the ministry. Mark 3:14 says,

> And He appointed twelve, that they might be with Him, and that He might send them out to preach.

It was only after the disciples had been *with* Him for some time that He began shifting some of the responsibilities for the ministry onto their shoulders.

---

3. For further study, consider the strategy Jesus used when sending out the disciples in Mark 6:6b–7.

Jesus' Delegation Analyzed and Developed

Now that we've had an overview of how Jesus guided the experience of the disciples, let's dig into that delegation a little more deeply with the help of three questions.

Why Was It Important?

Delegating the ministry to His disciples was important because Jesus knew He was leaving and the work had to continue. Christ talked about this all during His last meal with the disciples. And according to John 14:25–26, Christ even told them who would be there to pick up where He would leave off.

> "These things I have spoken to you, while abiding with you. But the Helper, the Holy Spirit, whom the Father will send in My name, He will teach you all things, and bring to your remembrance all that I said to you."

Also, since Christ was leaving and the disciples were staying, they needed to be equipped. In a prayer spoken while they were together in the Upper Room, Christ assures them that they have been equipped with everything the Father had given the Son.

> "Now they have come to know that everything Thou hast given Me is from Thee; for the words which Thou gavest Me I have given to them; and they received them, and truly understood that I came forth from Thee, and they believed that Thou didst send Me." (17:7–8)

Last, delegation was important because persecution was coming and the disciples needed to be ready.

> "These things I have spoken to you, that in Me you may have peace. In the world you have tribulation, but take courage; I have overcome the world." (16:33)

The constant thrust of Jesus' ministry with His disciples was realism. Through delegation, Christ was able to solidify their faith and prepare them for the difficulties that lay ahead.

What Were the Difficulties?

Practicing the art of delegation, humanly speaking, presented Christ with three problems. First, there was the difficulty of knowing

when to start delegating responsibilities to the disciples. It's a difficulty that refuses to conform to any standard answer because no
two discipling relationships are exactly alike. At best, we can note
that Christ didn't begin delegating until after the disciples had been
with him for a considerable amount of time.

Second, Christ faced the difficulty of letting go. Jesus loved His
disciples, whom He called His children, like any parents love their
family—but He even more. And no loving parents are eager to let
their children go out on their own, knowing that they will face
heartache and hostilities. Nevertheless, Jesus commissioned His
disciples to go (Matt. 10:5a). But with that commission He gave
them some advice, warnings, and reassurance.

> "And whoever does not receive you, nor heed your
> words, as you go out of that house or that city, shake
> off the dust of your feet. . . .
>
> "Behold, I send you out as sheep in the midst of
> wolves; therefore be shrewd as serpents, and inno-
> cent as doves. But beware of men; for they will de-
> liver you up to the courts, and scourge you in their
> synagogues; and you shall even be brought before
> governors and kings for My sake, as a testimony to
> them and to the Gentiles. But when they deliver
> you up, do not become anxious about how or what
> you will speak; for it shall be given you in that hour
> what you are to speak." (Matt. 10:14, 16–19)

Third, delegation involves being willing to risk mistakes and
failures. No child will ever learn to walk without falling in the
process. It's a part of growing up that every parent expects. And
what's true physically is also true spiritually. Jesus allowed His disciples to make mistakes and fail as they were learning how to walk
spiritually, because He knew it was a vital part of their maturation
process (see 17:14–20). Without this experience, the disciples
wouldn't have been ready to take on the Great Commission (see
28:19–20).

Where Did Delegation Lead?

When the Son returned to the Father, He left behind a band
of men who "turned the world upside down" (see Acts 17:6 KJV).
Men in whom the Spirit of God worked mightily to evangelize the
world, establish the church, and disciple others.

Delegation Applied Today

Let's turn from our study of Moses and Christ and focus now on how we can implement delegation today. What do you do when you sense it's time to push your disciple out of the nest to start serving others?

How Can It Be Implemented?

We can put delegation into practice in our discipling relationships by providing personal projects and practical work assignments. For example, have the person you're discipling begin to reach out to others through personal evangelism. Even better, take this person with you as you evangelize, to see firsthand how to do it.

At the appropriate time, we should also challenge the people we're discipling to begin praying that God would bring them someone to take under their wing to disciple.

Another good suggestion would be to encourage service in a local church. Being involved in this way will enable them to discover and cultivate their spiritual gifts.

But one of the best ways of getting disciples involved in ministry is simply to include them in your responsibilities. Wherever you go, take them with you so that they can observe and evaluate. Whenever a task of yours is too big, ask for their help, express your needs. Whatever you're struggling with, be open about it so that they can enter into your struggle with you.

What Must Be Remembered?

Guiding the discipling experience of another person is a tremendous responsibility. And there are some important principles that we need to remember. First, the negatives: As you begin discipling someone, don't overwhelm the person by starting too fast. A spiritual babe needs to be fed the milk of the Word before going on to more solid food.

Don't expect perfection. Nothing will kill another's spirit faster than unrealistic expectations. Set limited and obtainable goals so that the person can succeed and be stretched to go for more.

Finally, don't try to impress a disciple; focus on imparting. Disciples will find it next to impossible to follow a spiritual prima donna who fosters a facade of never having any problems or faults. But a disciple will eagerly follow the honest discipler who is open to sharing and talking about personal weaknesses and struggles.

On the positive side, remember to pass on every helpful thing you know. Be realistic and honest. And base all your delegation on three words: *Encourage—Encourage—Encourage!*

 ## *Living Insights*

Delegation can be such a bother.

Why didn't God just tell Adam the names of the animals instead of waiting on him to name them? Why didn't He just stamp "Made by God" under every leaf and rock instead of trusting that His followers would tell everyone of a holy and loving Creator? Why doesn't God just supernaturally tell the gospel to the whole world at once and be done with it?

C. S. Lewis said that God

> seems to do nothing of Himself which He can possibly delegate to His creatures. He commands us to do slowly and blunderingly what He could do perfectly and in the twinkling of an eye.[4]

You may be able to think of some reasons why God would voluntarily limit Himself this way; you could even ask a seminary student and probably learn a few more. But regardless of how many you come up with, they will never completely plumb the depths of this mystery: a God who is all-powerful and yet willingly delegates works of eternal consequence to you and me.

What's not a mystery is that you and I must also learn to delegate. There are those around us who need our help to mature in Christ. Certainly God could mature them perfectly and in the twinkling of an eye, but He chooses instead to disciple others by working through people just like us.

- To help you incorporate the practice of delegation in your discipling, think through the following areas and see if you can come up with some personal work assignments and projects that would help the person you're discipling grow in Christ.

Prayer: _____

_____

---

4. C. S. Lewis, "The Efficacy of Prayer," in *The World's Last Night and Other Essays* (New York, N.Y.: Harcourt Brace Jovanovich, 1960), p. 9.

Bible study: _____

_____

Evangelism: _____

_____

Service in a local church: _____

_____

Others: _____

_____

_____

_____

_____

Delegation a bother? No, it's a privilege.

>   *Help me, dear God, in my slow and blundering
>   ways to always strive to be a good and faithful steward
>   of this great privilege. Amen.*

 ## Living Insights

Have you ever had the kind of friend who would do anything
for you but would never allow you to do a thing in return? It's a
very frustrating relationship, really. One where you'll always be
treated as a child who needs to have everything done for it. It's a
one-way street that insidiously thwarts your every attempt to give,
practice your Christianity, and in short—grow.

Listen to a few of the ways physician and psychiatrist Paul Meier
describes how parents can raise healthy, normal children to become
drug addicts or alcoholics.

>   Make all of his decisions for him, since you are a
>   lot older and wiser than he is. He might make mis-
>   takes and learn from them if you don't. . . .
>
>   Always bail him out of trouble so he will like you.
>   . . . Never let him suffer the consequences of his
>   own behavior. . . .

Always step in and solve his problems for him, so he can depend on you and run to you when the going gets tough.[5]

Are you trying to disciple someone by doing everything for that person? Does your idea of discipling mean having all the answers, never being down emotionally, having no problems—life's just one happy lark with Jesus?

The word *suffocate* means "to impede or stop the development of."[6] Are you suffocating the person you're discipling? Are you depriving someone of the respect and responsibilities he or she needs to grow up in Christ? If you suspect that you just might be, take a moment to examine your discipling relationship with the following questions.

- Is it time in your discipling relationship to begin delegating?

  _____

- Are you willing to do that? _____

- What are some activities and responsibilities in your own life that the person you're discipling can be involved in?

  _____

  _____

  _____

If you're one who has trouble opening up to others and allowing them to really share in your life, read *The Trauma of Transparency*, by J. Grant Howard, or *Inside Out*, by Dr. Larry Crabb.

5. Paul D. Meier, *Christian Child-Rearing and Personality Development* (Grand Rapids, Mich.: Baker Book House, 1977), pp. 49–50.

6. *Webster's Ninth New Collegiate Dictionary*, see "suffocate."

Chapter 9

SUPPORT OF DISCIPLESHIP...
INTERCESSION

John 17:6–19

For millions today prayer has become a kind of Christianized Aladdin's lamp. You just decide what you want, rub the right kind of faith words, and God is at your command. One individual teaches,

> "You have to believe that those things you say— everything you say—will come to pass. That will activate the God kind of faith within you, and those things which you say will come to pass."[1]

In reality, however, there are no genies in lamps, and God doesn't always say yes to everything we ask for.

> I asked God to take away my pride,
>   and God said "No."
> He said it was not for Him to take away,
>   but for me to give up.
>
> I asked God to make my handicapped child whole,
>   and God said "No."
> He said her spirit is whole;
>   her body is only temporary.
>
> I asked God to grant me patience,
>   and God said "No."
> He said patience is a by-product of tribulation;
>   it isn't granted, it's earned.
>
> I asked God to give me happiness,
>   and God said "No."
> He said He gives me blessing;
>   happiness is up to me.[2]

1. As quoted by Bruce Barron in *The Health and Wealth Gospel* (Downers Grove, Ill.: Inter-Varsity Press, 1987), p. 103.

2. Claudia Weise, "God Just Says 'No.'" The poem was mailed to Bob Kraning, who is on the pastoral staff of the First Evangelical Free Church, Fullerton, California.

Not only do we not get everything we ask for, many of us need help in even knowing *what* to ask for. In our lesson today we will be studying how Christ prayed for His disciples, as recorded in John 17. And from this we will find some guidelines to follow when we pray for those whom God has given us to disciple.

The Emphases in Jesus' Prayer

Sometime between the Last Supper and the agony in the Garden of Gethsemane, Christ paused and earnestly prayed for His disciples. It was a prayer that the apostle John, huddled there next to Jesus, would never forget. Years later this disciple wrote down what he heard that night, leaving us the longest recorded prayer Jesus ever uttered to the Father.

Let's briefly look at the three major emphases in Christ's prayer.

Christ Prays for Himself

In the first five verses Christ refers to Himself ten times. The crux of His concern is summed up in John 17:4–5.

> "I glorified Thee on the earth, having accomplished the work which Thou hast given Me to do. And now, glorify Thou Me together with Thyself, Father, with the glory which I had with Thee before the world was."

Christ is filled with longing for the heavenly glory and splendor He shared with the Father before He came to glorify Him on earth.

Christ Prays for the Eleven Disciples

Beginning in verse 6, and going all the way through verse 19, the emphasis shifts from the Son to the eleven faithful men God gave Him.

> "I manifested Thy name to the men whom Thou gavest Me out of the world; Thine they were, and Thou gavest them to Me, and they have kept Thy word." (v. 6)

Christ Prays for Those Yet to Believe

And finally, verse 20 pivots our attention from the disciples to those yet to believe.

"I do not ask in behalf of these alone, but for those
also who believe in Me through their word." (v. 20)

The remaining six verses continue along this vein, as Christ
prays for the unity and destiny of all future believers.

Did you know that Jesus prayed for you that night? Did you ever
think about that? Jesus Christ remembered *you* in prayer, you who
were yet to believe on Him through the words of those who had
known Him personally.

The Disciples in Jesus' Prayer

Let's go back to Christ's second emphasis in His prayer, the
disciples, for a closer look at how we should intercede for the people
we're discipling.

His Personal Relationship with the Disciples

Verses 6–10 reveal the kind of relationship Christ had with His
disciples. Beginning with verse 6, we can see that Christ's relationship with the disciples was a godly one.

"I manifested Thy name to the men whom Thou
gavest Me out of the world; Thine they were, and
Thou gavest them to Me, and they have kept Thy
word." (v. 6)

He showed them the Father. When Jesus says that He "manifested"
God's name to His disciples, it doesn't mean that He simply told
them about God. To manifest something means to display it, make
it evident. The Jesus the disciples followed day after day was more
than just mere words about God, He was the embodiment of God.

He taught them to look to the Father. Another important aspect
of this relationship is that Christ trained His men to look to the
Father as the giver, the source of "every good thing bestowed and
every perfect gift" (James 1:17).

"Now they have come to know that everything Thou
hast given Me is from Thee." (John 17:7)

Christ didn't come to draw all the attention to Himself. Rather,
He wanted His followers to see and depend on the Father.

He emphasized the importance of God's Word. In the next verse
we'll see that Christ's relationship with the disciples was also cen-
tered around the Scriptures.

> "For the words which Thou gavest Me I have given
> to them; and they received them, and truly under-
> stood that I came forth from Thee, and they believed
> that Thou didst send Me." (v. 8)

It would have been easy for Christ to make His personality or His
works the center of the discipling relationship. Unfortunately, many
Christians have, and their disciples have been left starving for the
truth of God's Word.

He built an intimate friendship with them. Last, Christ's relationship with the disciples was unique; it was distinct from the relationship He had with the masses. It was up close and personal, a full
and intimate friendship.

> "I ask on their behalf; I do not ask on behalf of the
> world, but of those whom Thou hast given Me; for
> they are Thine; and all things that are Mine are
> Thine, and Thine are Mine; and I have been glori-
> fied in them." (vv. 9–10)

Jesus didn't pray for everyone. He prayed only for those eleven men
who followed Him. Theirs was a unique relationship, unlike any
that anyone had known up to that time.

His Personal Concern for Them

Christ's personal concern for His disciples, these men in whom
He has invested the last three years of His life, is now poured out
in three requests.

> "And I am no more in the world; and yet they them-
> selves are in the world, and I come to Thee. Holy
> Father, keep them in Thy name, the name which
> Thou hast given Me, that they may be one, even as
> We are. While I was with them, I was keeping them
> in Thy name which Thou hast given Me; and I
> guarded them, and not one of them perished but the
> son of perdition, that the Scripture might be ful-
> filled." (vv. 11–12)

First, *Jesus asks the Father to keep and to guard the disciples.* Up
until now Jesus has protected and preserved them against the evil
in the world. But now that He is about to leave, Christ places them
under the Father's care and protection. Notice the kind of protection Jesus asks for.

> "I do not ask Thee to take them out of the world, but
> to keep them from the evil one. They are not of the
> world, even as I am not of the world." (vv. 15–16)

Christ's prayer is not, "Isolate them"—take them out of the
world, but "Insulate them"—preserve them from the evil that sur-
rounds them. We cannot protect ourselves from evil by living behind the thick walls of a monastery or out in desert caves. What
we should seek, instead, is the refuge and protection God alone
can give in the midst of evil.

As a discipler, be committed to praying for the protection of
the person you're discipling. Don't ask God to remove temptations;
rather, pray that He will strengthen this individual to be able to
withstand them.

Second, *Jesus asks the Father to give them His joy.* With this point
Jesus requests something that many of us have never even thought
of praying about.

> "But now I come to Thee; and these things I speak
> in the world, that they may have My joy made full
> in themselves." (v. 13)

In the original text, the emphasis in this sentence is on the personal pronoun "My." Christ didn't ask that His disciples be joyful,
but that they experience *His* joy, a joy that provides a deep, inner
sense of contentment and peace. This doesn't mean Christians will
always have a grin on their faces and feel like laughing. Difficult
circumstances cross the Christian's path just the same as everyone
else's. The difference is that whatever the circumstances, the Christian can always possess a joy that is unshakably rooted in Christ.

Christ not only prayed for the disciples to have His joy, but that
this joy would be "made full." Someone whose joy overflowed was
the well-loved pastor Charles Haddon Spurgeon. At times he would
lean back and laugh out loud from the pulpit in London's Metro-
politan Tabernacle. When chided for this, he replied with a twinkle
in his eye, "If only you knew how much I hold back, you would
commend me."[3]

When you pray for a disciple, pray for that person's joy to be
made full. Pray that the pain and hurt of this fallen world will not
sour this growing Christian into someone who is cranky, stubborn,

---

3. As quoted by J. Oswald Sanders, *Spiritual Leadership,* rev. ed. (Chicago, Ill.: Moody Press,
1980), p. 84.

and discontented. There are already too many believers whose Christianity is about as joyful an experience as being a pallbearer at a funeral.

Third, *Jesus asks the Father to set them apart.*

"Sanctify them in the truth; Thy word is truth." (v. 17)

Sanctify means "to set apart for a divine task or purpose." Perhaps we can best see Christ's thought here by looking at the progression behind His requests. Jesus asked the Father to protect the disciples from the blows of a hostile world, to make their joy full, and now to set them apart in conformity to His truth. All this, so that they would be able to have the commitment needed to complete the job mentioned in verses 18–19.

"As Thou didst send Me into the world, I also have sent them into the world. And for their sakes I sanctify Myself, that they themselves also may be sanctified in truth."

As you pray, remember to ask God to sanctify the person you're discipling. Pray that the Lord would continue to set this individual apart in consecration to His Word and His service.

The Application of Jesus' Prayer Today

Stepping back from Jesus' prayer, we can see two important applications for us today.

What was true then is still true today. Jesus had a personal relationship with His disciples then, and He still does with those who follow Him today. And His personal concern is still the same "yesterday and today, yes and forever" (Heb. 13:8).

What was the task then is still the task today. Jesus asked His disciples to go and minister in a hostile world, and that is still our task today.

Are you busy at the task? Does anyone know about the Lord Jesus because of the perseverance of your faith? Because of your deep and abiding sense of His joy? Or because of your commitment to live according to God's Word?

An essential part of ministering in a hostile world is praying for those we're discipling. When you pause to pray with those you're discipling, remember to ask God to keep them, to make His joy full in them, and to sanctify them.

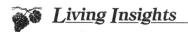

Let's take the three things Christ prayed for—protection, joy, and sanctification—and look into them a little more deeply in relation to the person you're discipling.

Keep Them

Is there a person or situation in your disciple's life right now that is still a strong influence toward evil?

_____

_____

Is the person you're discipling seeking protection from evil through isolation or through God's insulation?

_____

_____

Is this person blind to a particular spiritual danger?

_____

_____

Are you praying for God to protect this individual? Or are *you* trying to do this through your own efforts?

_____

Make My Joy Full in Them

Is there a particular area in which the person you're discipling seems unable to exhibit Christ's joy?

_____

Does this person understand the difference between happiness and Christ's joy?

_____

_____

What's needed to help this individual have Christ's joy?

_____

_____

Sanctify Them

If _sanctification_ means "to set apart for God's task and purpose,"
what are some of the major areas you see that are still not set apart
in the life of the person you're discipling?

_____

_____

_____

How will you go about helping this person give God control over
those areas?

_____

_____

_____

Is this individual's commitment strong, waning, or weak?

_____

Are there any obstacles that are keeping him or her from making
a firm commitment to follow Christ?

_____

_____

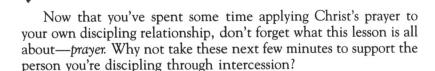 _Living Insights_   STUDY TWO

    Now that you've spent some time applying Christ's prayer to
your own discipling relationship, don't forget what this lesson is all
about—_prayer._ Why not take these next few minutes to support the
person you're discipling through intercession?

Chapter 10

ADVANTAGE OF DISCIPLESHIP ... EVALUATION

Selected Scripture

It has often been said that "Necessity is the mother of invention," and it could also be said that "Evaluation is the mother of improvement." With evaluation's help, things that need improvement become better, and things that are weak become stronger.

For example, if the car industry had stopped evaluating its product in the 1940s, we'd still be grinding gears, sticking to car seats in summer, and arm wrestling steering wheels.

Can you imagine what would happen to the space industry if they suddenly decided to stop evaluating?

> The enormous complexity of design, particularly of manned spacecraft, which involve literally millions of components, requires a high degree of miniaturization and achievement of reliability factors of over 99.9999 percent. An automobile whose parts had equivalent reliability would have a life expectancy of 100 years before its first malfunction.[1]

Without evaluation, there couldn't possibly *be* any space program. Nor would there ever have been an industrial, agricultural, or technological revolution.

Evaluation also affects our relationships. For years a good marriage was defined as one in which there weren't any problems. But all marriages have problems, and denying them only leads to more problems. It is only when two people face their problems and evaluate their major differences that their relationship can grow and become stronger.

Evaluation also plays an essential role in Christian growth. Many believers flounder for years without any significant spiritual growth because they lack the kind of objective, loving, biblical guidance necessary for improvement.

---

1. *Encyclopædia Britannica: Micropædia,* see "spacecraft."

In our lesson today we'll see that one of the most important advantages of discipleship is the way it invites evaluation. Jesus often injected this catalyst for growth into His conversations with the disciples. And with each dose, the disciples' childlike faith grew stronger and more mature.

Definition of Evaluation

For many today, having an evaluation feels the same as having your personal life run through a document shredder. Just the mention of the *e* word starts people biting their nails and fearing for their lives. But many of our fears are based on misunderstandings. So before we look at some examples of evaluation, let's formulate a definition of this precursor to improvement by briefly thumbing through the wisdom literature of Proverbs.

Timing

> Without consultation, plans are frustrated,
> But with many counselors they succeed.
> A man has joy in an apt answer,
> And how delightful is a timely word!
> (15:22–23)

One essential element of evaluation is timing. Of all people, counselors know the importance of a timely word. They know that wrong timing can completely defuse the impact of a word, even alter its meaning. To the wise parent, a well-timed word is a precious and powerful tool in raising children. In fact, in every good marriage or relationship you'll find people who are just as careful about choosing the right timing as they are about choosing the right words to express themselves.

Objectivity

> The first to plead his case seems just,
> Until another comes and examines him.
> (18:17)

The emphasis in this courtroom verse is objectivity. Whenever people plead their case before a jury, they present it from their point of view. But that's only one side. And it will probably sound as if it's the truth, the whole truth, and nothing but the objective truth. Complete objectivity, however, is rarely found in only one person's viewpoint. All of us need input from others to gain a more objective understanding of ourselves.

Guidance

> Prepare plans by consultation,
> And make war by wise guidance.
> (20:18)

Another important aspect of evaluation is guidance—receiving wise information. The context of the verse has to do with war, but wise guidance is something that all of us need in the broader context of dealing with life's situations.

Personal Interest

> Iron sharpens iron,
> So one man sharpens another. . . .
> As in water face reflects face,
> So the heart of man reflects man.
> (27:17, 19)

How is your inner person revealed and sharpened? Through another individual. If all you want to know is how you look on the outside, any mirror will do. But the best mirror for finding out what your inner person is like is a close friend.

Now let's piece together each of these nuances of evaluation for a comprehensive definition:

> Evaluation is a *timely* and *objective* appraisal given
> for *guidance* by one who is *personally interested* in you
> as an individual.

This definition gleaned from Proverbs also helps trim a few wrong ideas from our understanding of evaluation. Evaluation is more than just casual talk with someone else. And it's more than a stinging rebuke or a flattering compliment. It's an appraisal. One that may include a rebuke, advice, or a compliment. But always from someone genuinely interested in you.

Illustrations of Evaluation

Definitions are helpful, but sometimes *seeing* how things actually work in real life makes them easier to grasp. So let's look at three major realms of evaluation from Jesus' life, which we can apply in our own.

Sharing Insights

On several occasions Jesus prompted His disciples to make some improvements by sharing with them three types of evaluative insights.

Situational insight. Jesus often seized the moment in a situation to help the disciples recognize their needs. One example of this is found in Mark 6. The disciples have just reported back to Jesus after preaching and healing in the surrounding cities and villages.

> And the apostles gathered together with Jesus; and they reported to Him all that they had done and taught. And He said to them, "Come away by yourselves to a lonely place and rest a while." (For there were many people coming and going, and they did not even have time to eat.) (vv. 30–31)

Jesus listened carefully as each wide-eyed disciple related the wonders God had performed. It's possible that many of the men were anxious to go back out and continue preaching and healing. But beneath all the excited voices and dramatic reenactments, Christ saw that His men were exhausted. The most urgent need at that moment was for the disciples to balance their time of helping others with resting and being with Him.

Relational insight. Whenever we're experiencing a relational problem, insights from a close friend can help us know how to objectively evaluate and resolve the conflict.

In Mark 9:38 the disciples told Jesus about a relational problem they had encountered while out ministering.

> John said to Him, "Teacher, we saw someone casting out demons in Your name, and we tried to hinder him because he was not following us."

Many of us, especially new Christians, have a tendency to get locked into a spirit of independence, like the disciples did. We think that there's only one way of seeing things and all other ways are wrong. And we tend to exclude or oppose others if they aren't doing things the way we think they should be done. This kind of behavior only builds barriers in relationships, however, as seen in the disciples' actions. They could have welcomed this man as a fellow member of Christ's team, but instead they tried to hinder him, because "he was not following us." Christ responded with a relational insight that taught them to let go of their exclusivity and gave them a new criteria for evaluating others.

But Jesus said, "Do not hinder him, for there is no one who shall perform a miracle in My name, and be able soon afterward to speak evil of Me. For he who is not against us is for us." (vv. 39–40)

Personal insight. This particular kind of insight reveals the inner character of another person. Simon Peter received this kind of evaluative insight from Christ the first time he met Him.

One of the two who heard John speak, and followed Him, was Andrew, Simon Peter's brother. He found first his own brother Simon, and said to him, "We have found the Messiah" (which translated means Christ). He brought him to Jesus. Jesus looked at him, and said, "You are Simon the son of John; you shall be called Cephas." (John 1:40–42a)

Cephas, or Peter, means "rock." Christ saw a potential for strength and stability in Peter that this fisherman was probably not aware he possessed. The insights given to us by our friends, teachers, parents—even critics—are an invaluable tool for maturing our strengths and improving our weaknesses.

Identifying Blind Spots

Another way that Christ helped others to evaluate themselves was by pointing out their blind spots—problem areas in their lives that they weren't aware of.

Unwise statements. According to Luke 10:1–9, Christ appointed seventy followers to go out in His name to preach and heal. Later, when those same seventy disciples came together for a reunion, they had quite a few exciting stories to tell the Lord.

And the seventy returned with joy, saying, "Lord, even the demons are subject to us in Your name." (v. 17)

To Christ, the seventy's oohing and aahing over the power to cast out demons wasn't wise. They were intoxicated with this new power, which blurred their vision to the presumptuous attitude shared by all of them. So Jesus quickly sobered these followers, showing them their blind spot.

And He said to them, "I was watching Satan fall from heaven like lightning. Behold, I have given you authority to tread upon serpents and scorpions, and over all the power of the enemy, and nothing shall injure you. Nevertheless do not rejoice in this, that the spirits are subject to you, but rejoice that your names are recorded in heaven." (vv. 18–20)

Unrealistic opinions. As we saw earlier in our lesson, when Christ first met Simon, He called him Peter—the rock. Apparently the Lord saw rocklike qualities of strength and endurance in him. Sometime over the next three years, however, Peter developed an over-inflated opinion of his steadfastness.

Simon Peter said to Him, "Lord, where are You going?" Jesus answered, "Where I go, you cannot follow Me now; but you shall follow later." Peter said to Him, "Lord, why can I not follow You right now? I will lay down my life for You." Jesus answered, "Will you lay down your life for Me? Truly, truly, I say to you, a cock shall not crow, until you deny Me three times." (John 13:36–38)

Peter was sincere but totally unrealistic about his loyalty. And Christ was the honest friend who didn't allow this faulty opinion to go by unchallenged.[2]

Giving Direct Rebukes

People can get so fired up emotionally that it blinds them from being able to see people and situations from a godly perspective. Two of Jesus' disciples, James and John, felt this kind of white hot emotion, and it caused their reason to burn out of control.

And it came about, when the days were approaching for His ascension, that He resolutely set His face to go to Jerusalem; and He sent messengers on ahead of Him. And they went, and entered a village of the Samaritans, to make arrangements for Him. And they did not receive Him, because He was journeying with His face toward Jerusalem. And when His disciples James and John saw this, they said, "Lord,

---

2. Another blind spot is unbiblical goals. For an example of how Christ handled this with two of His disciples, read Mark 10:35–45.

87

do You want us to command fire to come down from
heaven and consume them?" (Luke 9:51–54)

Instead of rebuking the Samaritans with fire, however, Jesus
turned and rebuked James and John (vv. 55–56). Jesus knew they
needed to learn how to control their emotions to keep them from
responding in a blind rage every time someone criticized, insulted,
or misunderstood them.[3]

Techniques of Evaluation

Evaluation is a powerful tool. If wielded improperly, people can
be seriously hurt. But when used properly, it can become an incredible instrument for growth. Which way it will work for you will
depend on how well you apply the four key ingredients from our
definition of evaluation.

First: *Remember to choose your timing carefully.* Don't just dump
evaluations on other people. Plan ahead, use tact, and be sure that
you have developed the kind of relationship with this person that
warrants your giving this evaluation.

Second: *Stay objective.* Be sure that your evaluation is based on
facts, not hearsay. Also, don't let your love for this person cloud
your objectivity.

Third: *Guide them by expressing how your evaluation will benefit
them in reaching their goals.* Remember, your purpose is not to give
a static critique but to provide dynamic counsel that will provide
a path to the future for this person.

Fourth: *Say it with love.* You may be an expert at timing, objectivity, and guidance, but without a genuine concern for the other
person, you're not qualified to give an evaluation in the spirit of
Christ (see 1 Cor. 13:1–7).

 Living Insights STUDY ONE

A psychologist once said that the two hardest things to do are
to give up something old and take on something new. Perhaps that's
where most of the pain lies in receiving evaluations. We can fuss
about the evaluator's poor timing and prejudiced opinions, but what
really pains us is having to change.

---

3. For another example of rebuke, read Mark 8:31–33. See also Proverbs 27:6.

The essential nature of evaluations is to prompt change. And because of this, most of us try to nudge them out of our lives. It may not be something we do consciously, but the subtle direction of our lives is away from pain, not toward it.

Has someone ever shared an insight with you or revealed one of your blind spots that you need to go back and deal with?

_____

_____

Write out what you see about yourself that needs changing . . . and some practical ways for implementing a change.

_____

_____

_____

_____

_____

Giving up something that belongs to our old nature is not so painful when we focus on what we gain by being obedient to Christ. Paul had the right focus when he said,

> But whatever things were gain to me, those things I have counted as loss for the sake of Christ. More than that, I count all things to be loss in view of the surpassing value of knowing Christ Jesus my Lord, for whom I have suffered the loss of all things, and count them but rubbish in order that I may gain Christ. (Phil. 3:7–8)

 Living Insights   STUDY TWO

Evaluations can be used positively to stretch people to grow, or they can be used more like a medieval rack to simply inflict pain. Perhaps you've felt the pain of having your self-esteem pulled apart. We all have. And, yes, we've all succumbed to the same medieval temptation to put someone else through a Dark Ages evaluation.

An evaluation doesn't have to be a chamber-of-horrors device, however. With the help of Proverbs and the life of Christ, we now have the tools to dismantle our gruesome dungeon evaluations and replace them with evaluations designed to help others improve.

Is there someone you're discipling, a friend or family member, who needs an evaluation? _____.
What are the issues at stake?

_____

_____

_____

_____

When would be the best possible time to approach this person?

_____

Are you sure your viewpoint isn't based on a one-sided interpretation? Are there some points that still need clarification from this other person before you proceed?

_____

_____

_____

What particular guidance are you suggesting? Are there some specific biblical principles that you're using? Have you sought any second opinions about this?

_____

_____

_____

What are your motives for doing this evaluation? Are you seeking this other person's good?

_____

_____

Evaluations are hard work and they can be very emotionally draining. But if done right, at least this person will know that a friend—not an executioner—is doing the evaluating.

Chapter 11

GOAL OF DISCIPLESHIP...
REPRODUCTION

Selected Scripture

At the end of World War II, American soldiers came home to a world that was safe to raise a family in. And raise families they did. Boy, did they ever! The diaper decade of the fifties was the most fertile in America's history. Never before had couples been more fruitful or multiplied at such an explosive rate. However, the fuse to this population explosion was lit long before America was ignited by it—it first sparked in the Garden of Eden. Let's begin our study today by tracing this fuse back to its Old Testament origins.

Old Testament Parallel, from the Physical Realm

The beginning of this fuse is found in chapter 1 of the book of beginnings, the baby book of civilization—Genesis.

The Commands

The starting point we're looking for is found in the first recorded words that God spoke to Adam and Eve.

> And God created man in His own image, in the image of God He created him; male and female He created them. And God blessed them; and God said to them, "Be fruitful and multiply, and fill the earth, and subdue it; and rule over the fish of the sea and over the birds of the sky, and over every living thing that moves on the earth." (Gen. 1:27–28)

Isn't it interesting that God didn't say "Learn," "Work," "Enjoy," or even "Worship." He simply commanded them to do one thing— reproduce! Adam and Eve were to start a baby boom that would fill the earth with sons and daughters bearing God's image.

We know from Genesis 3, however, that Adam and Eve disobeyed another command of God, and that sin brought on spiritual death— separation from God—for themselves and all their offspring. Nevertheless, God didn't retract that first command. And Adam and Eve went to work multiplying and filling the earth. Unfortunately, their sin against God multiplied too, until God finally sent a flood to wipe out all of their children except Noah and his family. And what was one of the first things God said to Noah after the flood had dried up?

"Be fruitful and multiply, and fill the earth." (9:1b)

God lit the fuse for yet another baby boom with the same command—reproduce!

One of life's highest privileges and most exciting mysteries is wrapped up in this word *reproduce*. No matter whether we're rich or poor, famous or anonymous, educated or uneducated, God has endowed us with the powerful gift of co-creating with Him. And there are few desires stronger than our desire to use this gift, to see ourselves reflected in the tiny face of another living soul.

The Barriers

Physical reproduction is not always possible, however, for three basic reasons. First, we may lack a partner. Second, reproduction may be blocked because of a disease or other physical impairment. Or third, we may not be old enough—our bodies may not be mature enough to reproduce.

We've taken this time to trace God's command to reproduce and to examine the barriers that prevent fulfillment of that command because they provide a helpful parallel to the spiritual reproduction that takes place in discipleship.

New Testament Strategy, in the Spiritual Realm

When you cross over from the Old Testament to the New, you see that God's command to reproduce hasn't been rescinded, the emphasis has just shifted. The emphasis of the New Testament is not on physical reproduction, but on spiritual reproduction. We're to be reproducing after our own kind spiritually, and there is no better way to do this than by discipleship.

The Plan and Progression

Just as the fuse for the baby boom began in the first book of the Old Testament, the fuse for a future discipleship boom was sparked in the first book of the New Testament. From the very beginning, the goal Jesus emphasized as He called the disciples was reproduction.

And walking by the Sea of Galilee, He saw two
brothers, Simon who was called Peter, and Andrew
his brother, casting a net into the sea; for they were
fishermen. And He said to them, "Follow Me, and
I will make you fishers of men." (Matt. 4:18–19)

Luke puts it even more clearly.

And Jesus said to Simon, ". . . from now on you
will be catching men." (Luke 5:10)

Satan also has a plan for catching men (see 1 Pet. 5:8). Actually,
all people will either be caught for Jesus Christ or they will be
caught and used for the devil's purposes. So one of Christ's major
goals was to reproduce His life in the disciples, then train those
twelve men to catch others . . . who would in turn reproduce themselves spiritually in the lives of others . . . who would then begin
reproducing still more disciples.

This same emphasis is also present at the end of Jesus' earthly
ministry. Just prior to Christ's ascension, He issued the Great Commission to His disciples.

"Go therefore and make disciples of all the nations,
baptizing them in the name of the Father and the
Son and the Holy Spirit, teaching them to observe
all that I commanded you; and lo, I am with you always, even to the end of the age." (Matt. 28:19–20)

There is essentially only one command in all these words, and
that is to make disciples—reproduce. The Greek makes this even
plainer. The words "go," "baptizing," and "teaching," are all par-
ticiples that derive their force from one compelling and controlling
verb, "make disciples." Jesus' command echoes God's in Genesis 1,
only this time the emphasis is on spiritual reproduction. "Be fruitful,
multiply, and let the process continue until the whole earth is
filled—with disciples!"

Our mission as Christians is not simply to tell others about
Christ and then pack our bags and go home. We're to help lead
others to the Savior *and* nurture them to maturity so that they will
in turn multiply more disciples through this same process.

Did anyone take Christ's commission seriously? Yes. The whole
book of Acts describes the fruitful ministry of Christ's disciples.

A discipleship boom began on the day of Pentecost, and the number of new disciples continued to multiply geometrically.[1]

The Essentials and Enemies

Another area of close similarity between spiritual and physical reproduction is the kinds of barriers that affect both. Drawing from the barriers in the physical realm, we can find at least three reasons why we don't reproduce spiritually, and we can also find three essentials to overcoming these barriers.

Essential: union. Just as it is impossible to physically reproduce without a partner, so it's impossible to reproduce spiritually without being in union, in fellowship, with the Lord. John 15 says:

> "I am the true vine, and My Father is the vine-dresser. . . . Abide in Me, and I in you. As the branch cannot bear fruit of itself, unless it abides in the vine, so neither can you, unless you abide in Me. I am the vine, you are the branches; he who abides in Me, and I in him, he bears much fruit; for apart from Me you can do nothing. . . . By this is My Father glorified, that you bear much fruit, and so prove to be My disciples." (vv. 1, 4–5, 8)

Technically, the bearing of fruit in this chapter refers to the fruits of the Spirit blossoming in the life of a believer. But the principal emphasis is clear from this passage—apart from Christ we can do nothing, and that includes making disciples. If we join ourselves to Christ, however, we will produce fruit and it will be a fruit that lasts (see v. 16).

A powerful enemy of union is independence. A severed branch cannot bear fruit by itself. And in the same way, when we cut ourselves off from being in fellowship with Christ, our ability to reproduce spiritually withers and dies.

Essential: health. Christians who are not spiritually healthy will be unable to reproduce, just as someone who suffers from a disease or an impairment in the physical realm isn't able to do so.

In the parable of the sower and the seeds in Mark 4, Christ illustrates the need for health as well as the problem of disease. First, He tells the story of a farmer sowing seeds in four kinds of soil. Then He explains the spiritual significance behind the parable

---

1. See also Acts 2:41, 5:14, 6:1, 9:31, and 12:24.

to His disciples. The seed is the Word of God, and the different soils represent the different kinds of responses people have to the Word. In particular, let's note Christ's description of one response in verse 18.

> "And others are the ones on whom seed was sown among the thorns; these are the ones who have heard the word, and the worries of the world, and the deceitfulness of riches, and the desires for other things enter in and choke the word, and it becomes unfruitful." (vv. 18–19)

Perhaps it would not press the analogy too far to say that the worries of the world, the deceitfulness of riches, and the lust for other things are the diseases that will prevent us from being able to reproduce spiritually. We must constantly be on guard to weed out these attitudes from entwining around our hearts and strangling God's Word.

Essential: maturity. Physical reproduction is not possible without the necessary physical maturity, and neither is spiritual reproduction probable without a growing faith. In Paul's first letter to the Corinthian believers, he takes issue with their carnality, a prime enemy of maturity.

> And I, brethren, could not speak to you as to spiritual men, but as to men of flesh, as to babes in Christ. I gave you milk to drink, not solid food; for you were not yet able to receive it. Indeed, even now you are not yet able, for you are still fleshly. (1 Cor. 3:1–3a)

Paul had nourished the Corinthians with plenty of spiritual milk, so they should have matured. They should have been able to help nurture other newborn believers. But the Corinthians were still in spiritual diapers, because they were under the control of the flesh, not the Spirit.

Personal Application

There are two important applications for us to remember from our study today. First, *an unproductive life is an incomplete life.* If you're not in some way reproducing the life of Christ in others, your life will be incomplete. Second, *a productive life is a fulfilled life.* The most fulfilled Christians are the ones who are obeying Christ's commands, including the command to make disciples.

First and last words are often memorable ones. God's first words to Adam and Eve were "Be fruitful and multiply." And Christ's last earthly words to His disciples were "Make disciples." It's as though God is saying that our marching orders haven't changed, they've just shifted realms. In the beginning, His primary emphasis was on populating the earth through physical reproduction. Now it's on reaching that population through the spiritual reproduction of discipleship.

Are God's marching orders the emphasis in your life?

 Living Insights

As a discipler, sooner or later you're bound to be asked by a young disciple, "Where do disciples come from?" And then what are you going to do? Are you going to blush and pretend you didn't hear? Or are you going to be prepared to explain the "facts of spiritual reproduction?" In case you're feeling a little nervous and unsure about this, let's work on it together.

Here's something to get this important talk going. Basically, *the fact of life that will directly affect this disciple's capacity to reproduce other disciples in the future* is found in John 15:5.

> "I am the vine, you are the branches; he who abides in Me, and I in him, he bears much fruit; for apart from Me you can do nothing."

That word "apart" stands in direct contrast to the one word John uses ten times in this chapter—*abide.* What would help this budding disciple, perhaps more than anything else, is being taught how to abide in Christ. Take some time to study the following verses on abiding, then write your own definition of what it means to abide.

Psalm 15	1 John 2:3–6
John 8:31	1 John 3:9–10
John 15:1–10	1 John 4:9–16

_____

_____

_____

Hopefully you're beginning to feel a little more confident in your ability to handle this important subject. Just remember what you learned in the lesson, and don't be bashful about using your definition to explain things—you'll do fine.

 ## Living Insights

In his book, *Abide in Christ*, Andrew Murray asks,

> Who would, after seeking the King's palace, be content to stand in the door, when he is invited in to dwell in the King's presence, and share with Him in all the glory of His royal life?[2]

The answer: Nobody. But then why do so many Christians spend a good deal of their time standing in the doorway instead of in the presence of the King of Kings?

Take this time to examine your own life, looking for anything that might be keeping you from stepping past the threshold of that door. Is it one of the barriers to spiritual reproduction we talked about in our lesson? If so, write it down as specifically as you can, and map out a plan to pursue the essential that is necessary to get you through the door and into His presence.

Barrier: _____

_____

Plan: _____

_____

_____

_____

_____

2. Andrew Murray, *Abide in Christ* (Springdale, Pa.: Whitaker House, 1979), pp. 13–14.

Chapter 12

PROCESS OF DISCIPLESHIP... DEMONSTRATION

2 Timothy 2:1–10

OK, rookie, you're up!

For the past eleven lessons we've been working out hard to get you ready for this moment. Spring training is over. Now it's time for you to actually get in the game, be a player, start discipling someone, instead of discussing techniques on the bench. The "Disciple-the-World Series" (see Matt. 28:19–20) that Christ began still has several innings left to play. The Umpire who decides when it's time for theory to become reality is bellowing for you to "Play ball!"

The thought of actually taking a swing at discipling someone else, though, is a little scary . . . OK, a lot scary. You haven't even stepped up to the plate yet, and the pressure has you feeling light-headed.

One of the team's coaches senses you're having trouble. He's motioning for you to come over to him. It's Paul. You're glad to see a friendly face, even a scarred one like his. Paul got those scars when he was stoned and dragged out of the city of Lystra. Somehow those glazed patches of skin reassure you that he's been around the bases a few times and knows how you feel. If anyone can offer some good advice to settle you down, it's Paul.

So take a deep breath and listen up for four important principles this experienced coach wants to give you—batting tips that will help you get on base with this whole process of discipleship.

Principle One: Be Strong in Grace

> You therefore, my son, be strong in the grace
> that is in Christ Jesus. (2 Tim. 2:1)

Paul knows that few things are more winsome and refreshing than grace. It breathes life into all relationships, including discipling relationships. And Paul's encouragement to you is to be strong, literally "to be strengthened within"—let grace be reflected in your attitude. A practical way to do this is to give disciples room to grow through their failures and mistakes.

Perhaps another reason Paul wants you to be strong in grace is because there's no greater enemy to discipleship than legalism. The best way to strangle a growing disciple's enthusiasm is to force the person to fulfill to the letter what you consider to be vital Christianity. That's legalism. More specifically, it's marked by a rigid attitude of strict conformity to someone else's requirements in order to gain acceptance and respect. Christ said that His yoke was easy. Don't make it into a garrote with a lot of petty personal demands.

Principle Two: Be Investing Consistently in the Lives of Others

Next, Paul says,

> And the things which you have heard from me in the presence of many witnesses, these entrust to faithful men, who will be able to teach others also. (v. 2)

The word *entrust* that Paul uses here is a banking term. It means to "commit into a safe deposit." The idea is to deposit God's truth into the life of someone else where it will be safe, secure. Paul had already entrusted God's Word to Timothy, and now he wants Timothy to deposit it into the lives of several others. And those faithful disciples are to deposit the Word in the accounts of other faithful believers in an ever-multiplying transaction of discipleship.

How to Get Started Investing

How do we get started investing in the lives of others? Let's look at four specifics.

1. *Ask God to give you a sensitive spirit for identifying someone to disciple.*

2. *Be on the alert—don't scratch anybody off your list of possibilities.* Stay open.

3. *Reach out slowly and informally.* For example, invite someone out to lunch, a ball game, or the beach. Even better, find out what the other person enjoys most and give that a try.

4. *Before your time together is over, make specific plans to meet again.* As any member of the business world can tell you, if you simply say, "Let's get together again," chances are it won't happen.

What Investing Is Like

By this time you may be wondering what it's like to invest in others. Well, Paul is right in step with you, and in the next four verses he uses three pictures to explain what the process is like.

His first portrait is of a discipler in uniform.

> Suffer hardship with me, as a good soldier of Christ
> Jesus. No soldier in active service entangles himself
> in the affairs of everyday life, so that he may please
> the one who enlisted him as a soldier. (vv. 3–4)

Being in the military means giving up your own rights, and a discipler must be willing to do the same. Selfish people make poor disciplers. Also, being in the military means that you will be different from the majority—your goals and obligations will not be the same as a civilian's. In the same way, the goals and obligations of a discipler will set you apart from the majority of Christians who don't disciple.

Paul's next picture adds muscle tone and a sinewy determination to the discipler.

> And also if anyone competes as an athlete, he does
> not win the prize unless he competes according to
> the rules. (v. 5)

Every athlete knows that winning takes great discipline and consecration to the task. And it is the same with disciplers—only those people with commitment and discipline will make good disciplers.

Finally, with a last few brush strokes, Paul paints the discipler as a farmer.

> The hard-working farmer ought to be the first to
> receive his share of the crops. (v. 6)

Farmers' lives are full of hard, back-breaking work. But one of the benefits they enjoy is living off the crops they raise. Discipleship is also hard work. But one of the benefits of discipling others is that oftentimes they will be there to lend you a helping hand when you need it.

In short, investing in others on discipleship's terms will take an unwavering commitment to unselfishness, discipline, and hard work. But the payoff is eternal.

Principle Three: Personalize the Truths You Have Heard

> Consider what I say, for the Lord will give you under-
> standing in everything. (v. 7)

The word *consider* means "to perceive in the mind." Paul is suggesting, in addition to his three pictures in verses 3–6, that you make a mental picture from the things *you* have learned about discipleship. Don't clutter up your mind with images of how successful your pastor has been; think about your own life. Picture how you will actually start working with some individuals.

Maybe your most effective method of discipling will be as a married couple. You could invite others over for a meal and, if they become interested, expand that time to include some discipling.

If you live alone, you might prefer to work with people one-on-one. Or you could begin a small-group study. Another possibility is to meet with someone over breakfast or lunch once a week.

Have you ever considered ministering at a jail, a retirement home, or a hospital? What about the social clubs you're involved in? Is there someone there you see regularly? All of these are excellent places for starting up a discipleship ministry.

Get the picture?

Principle Four: Be Ready to Endure All Things

Last, Paul gives a reminder about two of the most important fundamentals in discipleship.

> Remember Jesus Christ, risen from the dead, descendant of David, according to my gospel, for which I suffer hardship even to imprisonment as a criminal; but the word of God is not imprisoned. For this reason I endure all things for the sake of those who are chosen, that they also may obtain the salvation which is in Christ Jesus and with it eternal glory. (vv. 8–10)

The first fundamental is: *Always train your disciples to keep their eyes on Jesus, not you.* If they get distracted from Christ by trying to be like you, they'll completely miss the fellowship and maturity only He can give them.

Paul's second fundamental is *endurance.* Go the distance. Be prepared to have your patience stretched to the limit. No one knows about this better than Paul. He was hated, stoned, beaten with whips and rods, shipwrecked, and more—but he kept going. He endured because every moment of his life was motivated by the purpose of enduring "all things for the sake of those who are chosen . . ." (v. 10a).

A Concluding Thought

One of the chosen whom Paul endured for was Dave Dravecky. Though separated by two thousand years, the tent maker and the ex-baseball pitcher for the San Francisco Giants are linked by thousands of other faithful disciples who have done and are doing exactly as Paul has instructed us to do today. To close our lesson, let's listen in as Dravecky describes how he obtained "the salvation which is in Christ Jesus and with it eternal glory" (v. 10b).

Working his way up through the farm leagues on his way to the majors was no picnic for Dravecky. And it was during this time that Dave attended some chapel services for the ball players. But the testimonies he heard didn't affect him much, as he explains.

> I didn't really need God. I'd always depended on my own abilities and my own drive, and I'd done pretty well with that. I thought of myself as a decent person. God received his due on Sunday morning. The rest of my life belonged to me.[1]

Still working his way to the majors, Dave was asked to play winter ball in Colombia, South America—twice. On the second trip his wife stayed behind in the U.S.

> With her so far away, the only solace I had was from a small bunch of players who were Christians and used to get together for fellowship. I'd sit in with them, not from any great conviction that I belonged, but just because I needed somebody to be with.[2]

Later, Dave was traded by the Pirates to San Diego, and that's when he met Byron Ballard, a baseball player and a discipler.

> He had brilliant red hair and freckles; he was tall with size fifteen feet. I liked the guy immediately. Everybody did. He seemed incredibly joyful about life. He had a wonderful, zany sense of humor.
>
> I saw some literature lying on his bed, Christian literature associated with baseball chapel. I commented on it and he asked me whether I was familiar with baseball chapel.
>
> "I sure am," I said. "I was the chapel leader in Buffalo."

1. Dave Dravecky, with Tim Stafford, *Comeback* (Grand Rapids, Mich.: Zondervan Publishing House; San Francisco, Calif.: Harper and Row, Publishers, 1990), p. 68.

2. Dravecky, *Comeback*, p. 72.

I saw Byron's eyes light up. He immediately assumed I was a born-again Christian, and made some kind of reference to that. I realized I needed to straighten him out. "I'm sorry," I said, "but there's no way. I really don't understand that terminology at all."

I suppose most people would have taken that as a rebuff, but Byron didn't. He kept talking to me. More than that, he got out a Bible and showed me where Jesus talked about being born again. (It's in John 3:3.) I was impressed. The guy obviously knew something. . . .

Byron didn't tell me his answers to my questions. He showed me answers in the Bible. For me that was very important, because I had no doubts that the Bible was true. I soon found out, through reading with Byron, that the Bible contained plenty of very understandable material. It gave me a perspective on God that turned my religious ideas upside down. . . .

I didn't become a believer overnight. I watched Byron like a hawk. And that drew me. It wasn't what he said that convinced me so much as the way he lived.[3]

"It wasn't what he said that convinced me so much as the way he lived." *Demonstration.* That's what the process of discipleship is all about.

 ## Living Insights STUDY ONE

In *Christian Psychiatry*, Frank Minirth's discussion on raising healthy children can help us understand the importance of demonstrating grace in discipleship.

> God gave us the example of how to produce healthy children when he chose that the foundation of a relationship between two individuals should be based on the concept of grace. Grace implies that the love of God is free and unmerited. Just as parents

3. Dravecky, *Comeback*, pp. 74–76.

usually accept their children and will have an innate love for them regardless of what they do, so God loves us. Although God does not always like our behavior, just as parents do not always like their children's behavior, there is a great difference between not accepting someone's behavior and not accepting him. Children still feel loved if parents do not accept their irresponsible behavior, but they feel rejected and discouraged if they feel that they themselves are rejected. This type of rejection leads to discouragement, neurosis, and even psychosis. Likewise, Christians may become discouraged, neurotic, or even psychotic if they feel their receiving or keeping Christ is conditional.[4]

If you are already a discipler, are you raising healthy disciples? Take some time to think through and evaluate your discipling relationship. Is it based on grace, reflecting Christ's unconditional love and encouraging growth? Or is it based on the tenuous tightrope of your pet do's and don'ts, stunting growth and destroying life?

_____

_____

_____

If it is based on the latter, humble yourself before God in prayer, and write down two practical ways in which you can change your discipling relationship so that it will become a pristine reflection of God's generous grace.

_____

_____

_____

If you are about to take your first swing at being a discipler, how do you plan to demonstrate grace in your discipling relation-

4. Frank B. Minirth, *Christian Psychiatry* (Old Tappan, N.J.: Fleming H. Revell Co., 1977), pp. 40–41.

ship? Brainstorm a few ways, and write them down so you'll have a strategic reminder for the days ahead.

_____

_____

_____

_____

_____

_____

🍇 *Living Insights* STUDY TWO

In Colossians 2:3, Paul says that in Christ "are hidden all the treasures of wisdom and knowledge." And for the past twelve lessons we have found many pearls of wisdom in our exploration of Christ's discipleship method.

Take a moment now to string together the pearls you discovered. Then write down how you will adorn your life with these precious jewels.

Place to Begin . . . Discipleship _____

_____

_____

Question to Answer . . . Is Discipleship Biblical? _____

_____

_____

Beginning of Discipleship . . . Selection _____

_____

_____

Curriculum of Discipleship . . . Association _____

_____

_____

Cost of Discipleship . . . Consecration _____

_____

_____

Stimulus of Discipleship . . . Impartation _____

_____

_____

Badge of Discipleship . . . Affection _____

_____

_____

Genius of Discipleship . . . Delegation _____

_____

_____

Support of Discipleship . . . Intercession _____

_____

_____

Advantage of Discipleship . . . Evaluation _____

_____

_____

Goal of Discipleship . . . Reproduction _____

_____

_____

Process of Discipleship . . . Demonstration _____

_____

_____

BOOKS FOR PROBING FURTHER

Y ou know how it is. You finish a lengthy study and you think you understand things pretty well. Then the minute you're out there applying things on your own, you suddenly have all kinds of questions.

Our time together has come to a close, but let me refer you to some other Christians whom you could hire for a slight publisher's fee to continue your education on discipleship and answer more of your questions.

Anders, Max E. *30 Days to Understanding the Bible*. Brentwood, Tenn.: Wolgemuth and Hyatt, Publishers, 1988. A disciple cannot practically serve the Master without a careful understanding of His instructions. In this book, Max Anders will help you gain a foundational grasp of the Bible's events, people, and concepts, integrating God's Word in an easy-to-understand overview. An ideal teaching tool.

Bridges, Jerry. *The Pursuit of Holiness*. Colorado Springs, Colo.: NavPress, 1978. Throughout our study we have caught glimpses of the bumpy path of one disciple in particular, Peter. He started as a rough-and-tumble fisherman who begged Christ, " 'Depart from me, for I am a sinful man, O Lord!' " (Luke 5:8), and ended as a faithful disciple who exhorted others to holiness: "Like the Holy One who called you, be holy yourselves . . . because it is written, 'You shall be holy, for I am holy' " (1 Pet. 1:15–16). Quite a challenge, isn't it? But if impulsive, imperfect Peter could do it, so can we; and Jerry Bridges' invaluable book will show us how.

Coleman, Robert E. *The Master Plan of Evangelism*. Old Tappan, N.J.: Fleming H. Revell Co., Power Books, 1964. This book examines Jesus' strategy of evangelism while He walked the earth, tracing His steps as revealed in the Gospels. Numerous ideas and illustrative points for this study guide and series of messages were derived from this fine little book. "It is must reading for all who desire to be engaged in an up-close-and-personal ministry with others."

Colson, Charles W. *Loving God*. Grand Rapids, Mich.: Zondervan Publishing House, 1987. The heart of discipleship is devoted, passionate love for God. In this best-selling book, also the winner of a Gold Medallion Book Award, Colson will call you to deepen your love and have a better, more committed relationship with our heavenly Father.

Crabb, Lawrence J., Jr. *Understanding People*. Grand Rapids, Mich.: Zondervan Publishing House, Ministry Resources Library, 1987. The discipling relationship is a very close and personal one, one that will require a discipler to have a depth of understanding, sensitivity, and wisdom. Larry Crabb's book will help you gain and sharpen these qualities in a framework that is strictly biblical.

Eims, LeRoy. *The Lost Art of Disciple Making*. Grand Rapids, Mich.: Zondervan Publishing House; Colorado Springs, Colo.: NavPress, 1978. In this book, the author looks at the growth process in the life of a Christian, from newborn to disciple to a worker for Christ. He also examines the nurture and guidance people need in order to develop into spiritually qualified workers in the Lord's church.

Gire, Ken. *Intimate Moments with the Savior*. Grand Rapids, Mich.: Zondervan Publishing House, Daybreak Books, 1989. In this sensitive devotional book, author Ken Gire provides portraits of intimate moments Jesus spent with individuals and how those instances changed their lives. His words will quiet your soul and train your eyes to look into the Savior's compassionate face . . . where you will learn to love Him.

Kincaid, Ron. *A Celebration of Disciple-Making*. Wheaton, Ill.: SP Publications, Victor Books, 1990. Rather than emphasizing personal evangelism, this book focuses on church-centered evangelism. The author proposes that reaching out by and through the church has the greatest potential for fulfilling Christ's commission to make disciples, and he shows lay people and church leaders how to take the initiative in this process.

McGinnis, Alan Loy. *The Friendship Factor*. Minneapolis, Minn.: Augsburg Publishing House, 1979. Discipleship is much more than just a teacher-student relationship. It is a friendship (see

John 15:15). In this book you will learn how to be a warmer, more lovable person; how to communicate better; and how to resolve tension. This is a must for a healthy discipling relationship.

Peterson, Eugene H. *A Long Obedience in the Same Direction.* Downers Grove, Ill.: InterVarsity Press, 1980. This is a classic book on discipleship—not concerned so much with making disciples as with being a disciple worthy of Christ's calling. Peterson looks to the Songs of Ascents, Psalms 120–134, to encourage fellow disciples to persevere in their faith.

Willard, Dallas. *The Spirit of the Disciplines.* San Francisco, Calif.: Harper and Row, Publishers, 1988. In his preface Willard writes, "The Spirit of the Disciplines is nothing but the love of Jesus, with its resolute will to be like him whom we love." *To be like Him whom we love*—that's our goal isn't it? This book will nurture the disciple's desire to be more like Christ.

Insight for Living
Cassette Tapes

DISCIPLESHIP
MINISTRY UP CLOSE AND PERSONAL

Discipleship involves ministering to other Christians one-on-one and showing them, through personal example, how to live the Christian life. But to disciple another, you must first be a disciple yourself—one who consistently puts God's will above personal wants and wishes.

The tough question for all of us who are serious about discipleship is, how do we practice it? If you are caught between the theory and the reality of ministry up close and personal, then this series is for you. Through it, you will not only discover workable principles and techniques, but you'll also learn how to apply them. Discipleship can then become an exciting part of your everyday living.

			Calif.*	U.S.	B.C.*	Canada*
DIS	CS	Cassette series, includes album cover	$36.66	$34.50	$49.44	$46.81
DIS	1–6	Individual cassettes, include messages A and B	5.31	5.00	7.18	6.79

*These prices already include the following charges: for delivery in **California,** 6¼% sales tax; **Canada,** 7% postage and handling; **British Columbia,** 6% British Columbia sales tax and 7% postage and handling. The prices are subject to change without notice.

DIS 1-A: *Place to Begin . . . Discipleship*—John 1:35–48; Luke 9:18, 23

B: *Question to Answer . . . Is Discipleship Biblical?*— Matthew 28:19–20; 2 Timothy 2:2; Acts 9, 11, 13–18

DIS 2-A: *Beginning of Discipleship . . . Selection*— Matthew 4:18–22; Luke 6:12–16; John 1:35–40; 6:66–68

B: *Curriculum of Discipleship . . . Association*— Selected Scripture

DIS 3-A: *Cost of Discipleship . . . Consecration*—Luke 14:25–35

B: *Stimulus of Discipleship . . . Impartation*— John 13:33–14:6, Mark 6:31–52, Luke 11:1–4

DIS 4-A: *Badge of Discipleship . . . Affection*—John 13:1-35

B: *Genius of Discipleship . . . Delegation*—Exodus 18:13–27; Matthew 9:35–10:19, 17:14–20

DIS 5-A: *Support of Discipleship . . . Intercession*—John 17:6–19
   B: *Advantage of Discipleship . . . Evaluation—*
      Selected Scripture
DIS 6-A: *Goal of Discipleship . . . Reproduction*—Selected Scripture
   B: *Process of Discipleship . . . Demonstration—*
      2 Timothy 2:1–10

How to Order by Mail

Simply mark on the order form whether you want the series or individual tapes. Mail the form with your payment to the appropriate address listed below. We will process your order as promptly as we can.

United States: Mail your order to the Sales Department at Insight for Living, Post Office Box 4444, Fullerton, California 92634. If you wish your order to be shipped first-class for faster delivery, add 10 percent of the total order amount. Otherwise, please allow four to six weeks for delivery by fourth-class mail. We accept personal checks, money orders, Visa, or MasterCard in payment for materials. Unfortunately, we are unable to offer invoicing or COD orders.

Canada: Mail your order to Insight for Living Ministries, Post Office Box 2510, Vancouver, British Columbia V6B 3W7. Allow approximately four weeks for delivery. We accept personal checks, money orders, Visa, or MasterCard in payment for materials. Unfortunately, we are unable to offer invoicing or COD orders.

Australia, New Zealand, or Papua New Guinea: Mail your order to Insight for Living, Inc., GPO Box 2823 EE, Melbourne, Victoria 3001, Australia. Please allow six to ten weeks for delivery by surface mail. If you would like your order sent airmail, the delivery time may be reduced. Using the United States price as a base, add postage costs—surface or airmail—to the amount of your order. Please use the chart that follows to determine correct postage. Due to fluctuating currency rates, we can accept only personal checks made payable in U.S. funds, international money orders, Visa, or MasterCard in payment for materials.

Overseas: Other overseas residents should mail their orders to our United States office. Please allow six to ten weeks for delivery by surface mail. If you would like your order sent airmail, the delivery time may be reduced. Using the United States price as a base, add postage costs—surface or airmail—to the amount of your order. Please use the chart that follows to determine correct postage. Due to fluctuating currency rates, we can accept only personal checks made payable in U.S. funds, international money orders, Visa, or MasterCard in payment for materials.

Type of Postage	Postage Cost
Surface	10% of total order
Airmail	25% of total order

For Faster Service, Order by Telephone

To purchase using Visa or MasterCard, you are welcome to use our **toll-free** numbers between the hours of 8:00 A.M. and 4:30 P.M., Pacific time, Monday through Friday, or our FAX numbers. The number to call from anywhere in the United States is **1-800-772-8888.** To order from Canada, call our Vancouver office at **1-800-663-7639.** Vancouver residents should call (604) 272-5811. Australia residents should phone (03) 873-3834. Telephone orders from other overseas locations are handled through our Sales Department at (714) 870-9161. We are unable to accept collect calls. FAX orders may be sent to (714) 773-9032 in the United States and (604) 271-3484 in Canada.

Our Guarantee

Our cassettes are guaranteed for ninety days against faulty performance or breakage due to a defect in the tape. For best results, please be sure your tape recorder is in good operating condition and is cleaned regularly.

Note: To cover processing and handling, there is a $10 fee for *any* returned check.

Order Form

DIS CS represents the entire *Discipleship . . . Ministry Up Close and Personal* series in a special album cover, while DIS 1–6 are the individual tapes included in the series.

Tapes	Unit Price Calif.*	Unit Price U.S.	Unit Price B.C.*	Unit Price Canada*	Quantity	Amount
DIS CS	$36.66	$34.50	$49.44	$46.81		$
DIS 1	5.31	5.00	7.18	6.79		
DIS 2	5.31	5.00	7.18	6.79		
DIS 3	5.31	5.00	7.18	6.79		
DIS 4	5.31	5.00	7.18	6.79		
DIS 5	5.31	5.00	7.18	6.79		
DIS 6	5.31	5.00	7.18	6.79		
				Subtotal		
		Overseas Residents *Pay U.S. price plus 10% surface postage or 25% airmail. Also, see "How to Order by Mail."*				
		U.S. First-Class Shipping *For faster delivery, add 10% for postage and handling.*				
		Gift to Insight for Living *Tax-deductible in the United States and Canada.*				
		Total Amount Due *Please do not send cash.*				$

If there is a balance: ☐ apply it as a donation ☐ please refund
*These prices already include applicable taxes and shipping costs.

Form of payment:

☐ Check or money order made payable to Insight for Living

☐ Credit card (circle one):   Visa   MasterCard

Card Number _____ Expiration Date _____

Signature _____
<small>We cannot process your credit card purchase without your signature.</small>

Name _____

Address _____

City _____

State/Province_____ Zip/Postal Code _____

Country _____

Telephone (____) _____ Radio Station ___ ___ ___ ___
<small>If questions arise concerning your order, we may need to contact you.</small>

Mail this order form to the Sales Department at one of these addresses:
Insight for Living, Post Office Box 4444, Fullerton, CA 92634
Insight for Living Ministries, Post Office Box 2510, Vancouver, BC, Canada V6B 3W7
Insight for Living, Inc., GPO Box 2823 EE, Melbourne, VIC 3001, Australia